For Teenagers Living with a Parent Who Abuses Alcohol/Drugs

For Teenagers Living With a Parent Who Abuses Alcohol/Drugs

Edith Lynn Hornik Beer

AN AUTHORS GUILD BACKINPRINT.COM EDITION

For Teenagers Living With a Parent
Who Abuses Alcohol/Drugs

AN AUTHORS GUILD BACKINPRINT.COM EDITION

Published by iUniverse.com, Inc.

For information address:
iUniverse.com, Inc.
5220 S 16th, Ste. 200
Lincoln, NE 68512
www.iuniverse.com

Originally published by Association Press

Credit for Graphic: Sheila Blume M.D.

ISBN: 0-595-15994-X

Printed in the United States of America

CONTENTS

Preface

FOR TEENAGERS LIVING With a Parent Who Abuses Alcohol/ Drugs is an updated version of the books *You and Your Alcoholic Parent*, first published in 1974 by Association Press, and *A Teenagers Guide To Living With An Alcoholic Parent*, published in 1984 by Hazelden Educational Material. The original book was written with the encouragement of the late Dr. Frank Seixas (at that time medical director of the National Council on Alcoholism). Because of the variety of substance abuse, NCA has since changed its name to National Council on Alcoholism and Drug Dependence Inc.

The purpose of this new book, *For Teenagers Living With a Parent Who Abuses Alcohol/ Drugs,* is to include all substance addictions — not just alcohol. No matter whether a teenager lives with a parent who is an alcoholic, cocaine, crack, heroin, tranquilizer, or marijuana abuser or who suffers from cross addictions, the pain, the family trials, the hurt are still all there. This book will discuss how young people living in such a family can help themselves.

Edith Lynn Hornik-Beer

Introduction

THIS IS A book for those of you who are living with a drug-dependent parent or parents. This includes alcoholism. You are well aware of the emotional impact your parent's drug dependencies has on you and the perplexities, difficulties, and abuses you are faced with. You are probably seeking more information on how to manage your lives under such circumstances. You may wonder whom you can turn to and if they will understand the fear you live with at home. You worry whether your parent will be abusive. Will he or she pass out? Will your mother forget to turn off the stove when alone in the house? Will you face another lonely evening because your father sits in glum silence with his liquor bottle or his pills as his sole companion?

In writing this book it has been my object to define in realistic, concrete, and non-technical language the essential facts of alcoholism and other drug dependencies and what you, as a young person, experience under such circumstances.

For many years I have had the opportunity to teach creative writing and to write for teenagers. My writing led me to wherever young people might be: The Youth Consultation Services, teenage walk-in centers, Family Service, hospitals, Alateen, police headquarters, courts, and all kinds of schools — private, parochial, and public.

Whenever a real problem came up, such as a teenager dropping out of school in despair or turning to hard drugs in anger and pain, too many of the cases could be traced to serious problems in the home. Those who came from drug-dependent homes showed signs of being abused, mistreated, and often neglected. They were subject to mental depression and had feelings of guilt and inferiority. All too many had not been helped to recognize that their immediate personal difficulties related to the parental addiction at home. These youngsters knew only that they had lost confidence in themselves, in the community, and in their parents. But once the source of the problem was discovered, they wanted more and more answers to what was going on in their home, and with the answers came a certain amount of relief from the disruption of their lives.

This book is a composite record of all those questions young people have asked in my presence and is based largely on their experiences with parental alcoholism, drug abuse, and cross addiction.

I have attempted with a question and answer format to get down to such practical problems as: How can I change the situation, or how can I help? How can the family get help? How do I bring a friend home when my parent is drunk? What do I do if my doped up parent hits me or insults me unfairly? No matter how upsetting these problems are to you personally, they all tie in with the fact that drug dependency is a disease: the substance abuser is a sick person, and you are affected by his or her illness.

It's important to know that you are not alone. The United States Public Health Service ranks drug abuse — along with heart disease, cancer, and mental illness — as one of the great health problems in the country. There are separate statistics for each drug — heroin, cocaine, marijuana, etc. For example, it is estimated that close to a million people need treatment for heroin addiction. About eleven million abuse marijuana. There are over ten million alcoholics in the United States. Think of it — there are enough alcoholics or marijuana users in the United States to form a small nation. Switzerland has a population of seven million and Denmark has five million.

If you count only the sons, daughters, husbands, and wives affected by living with alcoholics, plus the marijuana users, the number of those hurt multiplies into the eighty millions.

The answer to living with drug addiction, as it is to any other disease, is knowledge. It may bring you new hope, courage, and peacefulness.

Acknowledgments

THE UPDATING OF the present book, *For Teenagers Living With a Parent Who Abuses Alcohol/ Drugs,* was done with the help of Sheila Blume, M.D., F.A.T.A., F.A.S.A.M. and former Director of New York State Division of Alcoholism and Alcohol Abuse, and Nicholas A. Pace, M.D., F.A.S.A.M. Among other honors, Dr. Pace is a Life Member of the National Council on Alcoholism and Drug Dependence, a Fellow of the American Society of Addiction Medicine and New York Academy of Medicine. He was adviser to First Lady Nancy Reagan for the Chemical People Project.

Others who went out of their way to help make this book possible are Melody J. Anderson, C.S.W., counselor/therapist and coordinator of Family Services at Hazelden New York; Naomi Weinstein, director of Children of Alcoholics Foundation, an affiliate of Phoenix House; Don Fass, executive director of Streetcats; Terry Paine, NCADD, Family Education Services Coordinator; Angela T. Zinzi, MSEd, Campus Outreach Coordinator, Children of Alcoholics Foundation; Brian Johnson of NCADD in Kansas City; Alfred Hellreich, M.D.,F.A.A.D., Joan Steingart, C.S.W.

Editor's Note:

THE PRONOUNS HAVE been alternated throughout the text in order to avoid the cumbersome use of he/she. This should in no way imply stereotyping of any behaviors to either sex.

1

Alcoholism and Other Substance Abuses

IF ALCOHOL IS a drug why list it separately from other addictive drugs?

Alcohol can be obtained legally and without a prescription. Social drinkers or people who occasionally have one or two drinks are usually not affected adversely.

What is alcoholism?

Alcoholism is a disease of the body, mind and spirit. Alcoholics are as sick as people who have tuberculosis or diabetes. People who are alcoholics are excessive drinkers. They cannot always stop at one or two drinks. Most alcoholics start out with the same intentions as the nonalcoholic: to have no more than one or two drinks. The nonalcoholics, or so-called social drinkers, can stop when they choose. Alcoholics cannot. For alcoholics, drinking becomes a compulsion. They are victims of their own compulsion. They will drink to quiet their nerves, their unhappiness, or to avoid making an important decision.

My father drinks only on weekends. Is it the number of times a person drinks each week or the quantity of alcohol consumed that describes an alcoholic?

Neither. There may be periods — weeks or months — when an alcoholic does not drink. The important point is that when alcoholics drink they lose control of their actions. The drinking may eventually damage them physically and mentally. It can keep them from performing their job and from getting along with family and with neighbors.

If alcoholics know they can't drink, why don't they just get hold of themselves and stop drinking?

It is a physical and not a moral illness. The body metabolizes the alcohol poorly, but the mind tells the alcoholics that they can drink. Their spirits tell them they need to drink to handle their fears and anxities.

I feel if I could just keep my father from seeing alcohol he would give it up. Should I throw out all the bottles in the house?

Teenagers have wanted to throw out the liquor in the house or ask friends not to drink in the alcoholic's presence. This will not solve the problem. You cannot prevent the alcoholic from coming close to alcohol any more than you can prevent a diabetic from seeing sweets. The problem is within the person and not in that bottle of alcohol.

How does drug addiction start?

Drug addiction can start in several ways. Sometimes it can start by taking prescription drugs for other reasons than for what they were prescribed. For instance a doctor may prescribe codeine after a painful surgery. The patient may like the dreamlike sensation and continue to take the prescription when no longer needed. I know of one woman whose mother was dying of cancer. The daughter "shared" her mother's pills. By the time the mother died the daughter had become addicted to pills.

A person may become an addict if she takes drugs regularly to forget a problem, to quiet unpleasant, nagging feelings, to calm nerves or to feel more adequate in social or work situations. Addicts become nervous and unhappy and lose control over their lives and actions. Whatever the reason they are unable to stop at will.

If the alcoholic or a drug addict needs help, why doesn't she go to a doctor?

In the early stages of addiction, addicts are usually not aware they are ill. Addiction is a progressive illness. Even when the addict becomes aware that all is not well, she may still be the last one to connect the illness with drug taking or drinking. It is this denial that keeps the addict and her family locked into the illness.

Why do some people vomit when they take drugs or drink alcohol?

Alcohol and drugs may irritate the lining of the stomach. It is this irritation that causes the gagging, nausea, and vomiting. There also can be an effect on the vomiting center in the brain.

What is meant by "passing out"?

Passing out is a loss of consciousness.

What causes this loss of consciousness?

Some drugs, including alcohol, sedate the brain and when taken excessively can cause a loss of consciousness and even death. Mixing drugs, including over-the-counter medication, can amplify the adverse effect.

The family of a drug abuser should be aware that mixing drugs can cause a person to pass out or, in some cases, death may result. For instance sleeping pills or tranquilizers, since their effect lasts longer when mixed with alcohol, can cause an alcoholic to pass out. Such a situation might be very serious even if he is used to alcohol. Furthermore, certain metabolic conditions such as diabetes or cirrhosis of the liver can cause unconsciousness even without alcohol or other drugs. It is good for everyone in the family to know if the substance abuser has such an illness so that if he were found unconscious, the family would be able to inform the attending doctor.

What is a blackout?

Some substances such as heroin or alcohol may cause temporary loss of memory.

For instance, when a heroin addict is in withdrawal, she may not remember the last four or five days.

In other cases, when a person drinks heavily and steadily and the brain becomes adapted to alcohol, she does not become unconscious as quickly as you or I would. In fact, she may act in a perfectly sober manner, but will have periods of time during which she has a loss of memory. Blackout is the term used to describe this temporary loss of memory.

Unless you have a reason to ask the addict if she remembers, you have no way of knowing whether she had a blackout. Sometimes the substance abuser will attempt to cover up for this memory loss because it is embarrassing. Usually the loss of memory is total and she will completely dispute the events that took place while the blackout was occurring.

While driving a car, the substance abuser may have hit another car and not remember the accident. If you know about blackouts, you will understand that this person is probably being as honest as she can when saying, "I don't remember." You will just have to accept this answer as the truth.

Do certain types of families tend toward substance abuse?

We know from studies that alcoholism and substance abuse may be hereditary. There are studies of children born to alcoholic families who were adopted as babies by nonalcoholic parents. Their rate of alcoholism was compared to children whose biological parents were not alcoholic, but were also adopted as infants. When these adopted children's adult years were carefully followed, it turned out that the children whose biological parents were alcoholic had much higher rates of alcoholism, even though they had not been raised by alcoholic parents.

Doctors are also gaining more insight into how we metabolize alcohol and other drugs. Some people metabolize drugs and alcohol more quickly than others. Furthermore, people have various levels of serotonin, a chemical related to our sense of energy, and dopamine, related to our sense of happiness. There are those who instead of exercising, socializing, or doing hobbies try to make themselves "feel good" and "raise the energy" with alcohol and/or drugs. Of course, we also hear of some in competitive sports who feel so tense that they take drugs to loosen up, feel better and perform better. Unfortunately, these substance abusers turn out to have problems with these chemicals.

Does this mean that I will suffer from substance abuse?

We are all susceptible to addiction. According to statistics, if you have at least one parent who is a substance abuser your chances of becoming a substance abuser is three to four times that of the general public, and that includes eating, gambling, and compulsive shopping. You need to be extra careful. It is similar to other diseases. Say you have a mother who became diabetic in her adult years, you will tell your doctor to check your blood sugar and you yourself will watch your diet.

Many young people simply do not experiment with any harmful drugs. They make friends with those who do not do drugs, because when you are around teenagers who abuse substances it's easy to copy those unhealthy ways to deal with feelings. Teenagers who refuse to do drugs meet people by joining groups that go hiking, dancing, do volunteer work, or are active in their church or synagogue. They join their drug-free friends' families for dinner and outings. This is discussed in greater detail in Chapters 9 and 14.

My parents are in treatment for addiction. My mother is a heavy marijuana smoker and my father likes to drink several six packs of beer in one evening. I went to counseling with them. My mother said she started smoking pot in high school and my father said that he started drinking beer in seventh grade. In my school I have noticed kids in fifth grade sniffing glue, and some smoking cigarettes. Are kids starting today at a younger age?

When compared to thirty years ago, more young people are drinking and experimenting with drugs at an earlier age. Counselors have noted that most who end up with addiction start out with a cigarette, then try alcohol ("just a beer"), and continue on to marijuana and cocaine.

My parents' counselor said that my father's drinking was already excessive and acute when he was a teenager. What is excessive and acute alcohol use?

There are different drinking habits among teenagers. Some teenagers drink regularly. Other teenagers and youths may drink less regularly, but when they drink they tend to consume larger amounts. These large amounts (or excessive and acute alcohol use) cause acute problems ranging from traffic fatalities to other alcohol-related injuries. Furthermore, both the teenagers who drink regularly and those who drink occasionally but excessively make themselves sick and are often impaired and unable to concentrate. Their drinking habits may keep them from completing their education and reaching the goals they desire.

Is this binge drinking?

Binge is a spree, a nonstop drinking or drugging party. This is extremely dangerous and can cause death.

I experimented with some drugs and found I actually liked it. Does that mean I am at risk even though I was only experimenting?

Yes. Be aware that your compulsion to experiment is a bio-chemical risk. When you take alcohol or drugs because it makes you feel better, it will in the end magnify your pain and leave you feeling worse. If you are truly taking drugs or alcohol, join Alcoholics Anonymous, Narcotics Anonymous or one of the other groups listed at the end of this book.

Do all teenagers experimenting with pot and alcohol become drug abusers?

Some "mature out" and do not become problem drinkers or drug abusers. A recent study has shown that adolescents with "prob lem behavior" have a higher risk of becoming substance abusers as adults.

What is "problem behavior"?

Problem behavior may include alienation from school, teachers, religion, or positive moral beliefs. Other problems include use of alcohol and other drugs and inappropriate sexual behavior. Teenagers who seek help from counselors or religious groups in order to deal with their problems and set goals for themselves may change their whole life in a positive way. Sometimes teenagers whose problem behavior does not get them into grave consequences may not take their problems seriously enough.

I do smoke pot occasionally. Does that make me an addict?

Ask yourself the following questions:

1) Is drinking or drug abuse affecting your reputation in school?
2) Do the kids you hang around with use drugs or drink in order to have fun?
3) Do you take time from school and homework so that you can drink or do drugs?
4) Are you frequently absent from school because you are sleepy or don't feel well?
5) Do you drink or use drugs because you are shy with other people?
6) Do you ever drink or use drugs alone? Smoke pot alone?
7) Is there a special time you do drugs or drink, such as Saturday nights or after school?
8) Do you use drugs or drink to avoid worrying or to calm your anger?

If you are worried about your drug habits or answered yes to any of these questions you should see a counselor or seek out Narcotics Anonymous or Alcoholics Anonymous. For further information you may want to look up some of the groups on the Internet listed at the end of this book.

Is using alcohol with marijuana dangerous?

Using alcohol and marijuana together is twice as dangerous as only drinking. Tests have shown that abilities and health were more impaired with alcohol and marijuana combined than with either drug alone.

What about using marijuana alone? My parents said they used marijuana when they were in school and still do now on weekends. They say that marijuana has medicinal properties and should be legalized.

Marijuana is a complex Hemp plant. Its risks outweigh its benefits. People who are addicted to marijuana may rationalize that it has a mild anti-nausea effect and some properties that may counteract glaucoma. However, the inhaled dose cannot be controlled and the side effects are dangerous. Pharmacies have excellent anti-nausea medicine and prescriptions to control glaucoma with fewer side effects.

Isn't it true though that on the whole marijuana is better than alcohol?

No, marijuana does not leave the body quickly. Alcohol is water-soluble. One ounce of alcohol is completely metabolized to water and carbon dioxide in two hours.

The difference between an occasional drink and an occasional joint is that you know exactly what is in a bottle of alcohol and that it is a legal drug.

A bottle of alcohol is labeled under government regulations with all of its ingredients.

The grass that comes from Mexico is different than grass from Asia or grass grown in the United States. Therefore, you are at the mercy of the one who sells or gives you the joint. Very often the seller or someone who gives you a joint has no way of knowing what strength or what type of grass is offered. You also don't know what pesticides were sprayed on the leaves.

Marijuana stays for days in your fatty tissues, including in your reproductive organs and the brain. Marijuana can impair your ability to drive a car, study, work, and in general reduces your energy. Marijuana draws people into an altered lifestyle and a dependence on a drug lifestyle. T.H.C., is the main active chemical in marijuana, accounts for most of marijuana's psychoactive/mind-altering effects. When marijuana is taken frequently there is a high accumulation of T.H.C. in the body since a single dose of T.H.C. takes thirty days to be completely eliminated.

Marijuana has more than four hundred known chemical toxins, and when burned, still other toxic compounds are produced. Tests have shown that chronic marijuana smoking can cause cellular damage. Tar from marijuana painted on the backs of animals has caused cancer. Marijuana can damage your immune system. It produces chronic irritation of nasal and lung passages. It suppresses the sex drive and can lead to erectile impotence.

If you are feeling down is it less dangerous to take prescription tranquilizers?

All drugs can be dangerous and addictive unless carefully prescribed by a physician. One physician in the field of substance abuse has called careless pill taking "eating your drug abuse."

My mother takes tranquilizers. She has been in car accidents and tends to sleep most of the day. It's like living with someone who isn't "completely here." I phoned my aunt, who said my mother's physician is prescribing mild pills while she is going through her divorce and is in counseling. I don't know what to do.

First of all your mother may have pills from more than one doctor. She can go to an internist and say, "I am sleeping poorly. I am sure it is just temporary." She may repeat the same statement to her gynecologist and her psychiatrist. She may be filling her prescriptions in different pharmacies. And she may not even be keeping them in her bathroom medicine cabinet. Try and notice when your mother's mind is clear — perhaps when your mother wakes up from her nap or in the morning. You may then want to tell her that you are worried about her. Tell her that you miss her old self. You may also want to phone each of her doctors and tell them what you have noticed and see if she is getting more than one prescription. You are for the moment not getting the parenting you need. You should discuss this with your own counselor who may suggest that you move in temporarily with your father, aunt, or whoever can provide you with a supportive home. You can get further aid by picking one of the help resources such as Narcotics Anonymous listed in the last chapter of this book.

What can one do if one feels bad? What is wrong in taking a tranquilizer to feel better?

Any tranquilizer needs to be administered carefully by a physician to make sure the patient does not become addicted to the prescription. Furthermore, the patient needs to find out what is making him feel bad. Is there a physical problem caused by a biological imbalance?

Counseling is very important. Don't forget joining and following Narcotics Anonymous Twelve Step program, which help all substance abusers, has saved many a life. The support the addicts give each other in these groups has given hope and strength to many a discouraged person. And, those living with the substance abuser have helped their lives by joining such organizations as Nar Anon Family Groups, or Families Anonymous. There are over thirty organizations geared to teenagers. These are listed in great detail in Chapter 14.

Very often the person will learn that a change of lifestyle can help. Instead of sitting and taking drugs, getting out and participating in a self-help group, taking a brisk walk, going swimming, playing basketball, or joining a community group such as a theater group can uplift one's spirits.

Why do some people become addicted, while others who take an occasional drink or an occasional tranquilizer or cough medicine can just stop?

Scientists have made the case that the dopamine area in our brains–known as our pleasure center–seeks an elevation of dopamine and it is this surge that triggers in addicts the so-called "high." However, there are better ways of stimulating our dopamine, such as working out, listening to music, tasting good food, a kiss.

Addicts do not crave heroin or cocaine or alcohol or nicotine per se, but want the rush of dopamine that these drugs produce. Scientists wonder if some people's bodies might produce too little dopamine and cause them to seek a "high" from drugs.

Very simply put, dopamine is a transmitter that ferries messages from one nerve cell (neuron) within the brain to another. To complicate matters, drugs alter many pathways and have horrible side effects. These include mood swings, impaired judgment and verbal ability, inability to concentrate, deterioration of relationships with family and friends. Drugs can damage the liver, pancreas, respiratory system and immune system.

2

Are You Sure You Have a Substance Abuser in Your Family?

ARE ALL ILLEGAL drugs bad even if taken in moderation? And who decides they are bad?

In this country and many other countries drugs are tested carefully by scientists for our protection. The results are released to physicians and to the public. You can read about all drugs in the library and on the Internet. Illegal drugs are dangerous to your health and that is why they are illegal.

Alcohol is legal. Is all drinking bad?

Not all drinking is bad, nor does all drinking lead to alcoholism. Many people drink to be sociable. They may have one or two cocktails before dinner. Or they may have a few drinks at a party to relax. But they know when to stop, and they have no trouble stopping. They may occasionally have one too many, but their drinking is not continual or habitually excessive.

Others drink to enhance their eating experience. Many a gourmet would not touch a roast beef without the proper accompanying glass of red wine, nor would she consider a good fish dinner complete without the correct white wine.

Some nations take pride in their national drink. Germany is associated with beer, France with wines and champagnes, and Russia with vodka. When traveling, many tourists enjoy each country's drink without any harm to themselves.

Some of us are accustomed to seeing alcohol used in religious rituals. It's interesting to note that alcohol was one of the earliest forms of medicine.

How can I tell if my parents are really alcoholics or if I am only imagining they are drinking too much?

To gain more insight into your family's drinking ask yourself the following questions:

1. One or both of my parents have alcohol on their breath before 10 AM

2. One or both of my parents do not bother to eat regular meals and drink instead

3. One or both of my parents do not remember what they said or did or what happened to them after they slept off the effects of their drinking.

4. One or both of my parents do not spend time mixing cocktails or comment on how the drinks taste but gulp down many drinks straight.

5. One or both of my parents have to take a drink when asked to make a decision.

6. One or both of my parents, on occasion, stay intoxicated for several days.

7. One or both of my parents get intoxicated on working days.

8. I discover hidden bottles of alcohol in the most unlikely places in our home such as under a pillow, behind the couch, or in the bathroom.

If you reacted with a "yes" to one or more statements, you may have someone in your home with the symptoms of alcoholism and/or substance abuse.

Because alcohol is used socially and is a legal drug, observing other drugs is so different. How can I tell if my parents are really some sort of other substance abusers or if I am only imagining it?

Just wondering may mean you have some sort of problem at home. Remember that not all problems are drug related. For example a parent could be angry and abusive without taking drugs. These are problems that must also be solved but they are not drug related.

If you are not sure if your parent is taking drugs ask yourself the following questions:

1. Have you actually seen your parents smoke marijuana, sniff a powder, or ingest an illegal drug such as cocaine or heroin?

2. Have you ever joined your parents in smoking pot or drinking just to keep them company?

3. Have you noticed your parent taking pills from various
    bottles and becoming unnaturally sleepy or having a com-
    plete mood change?

4. When you ask your parent what drug she is taking are you
    met with anger?

5. Does your parent blame you for taking drugs–"if you kids
    weren't so noisy"–"if you kids got better marks in school"—?

If you answered "yes" to any of these questions you may have a
serious drug abuser in the family.

**Is there a particularly good time to discuss my concerns with my
parent?**

It is difficult to tell a person he is a substance abuser if he has not
yet realized it himself. If you start to diagnose your parent's illness, he
might feel you are acting out of place. Thus, without meaning to,
you might hurt his feelings and affect your future relationship. Most
important, if the substance abuse your parent uses makes your parent
moody and angry you might endanger yourself.

When a parent drinks or is taking any other drug, try not to get
into a conversation. Anyone who is under the influence of a drug
won't know what he is saying or doing. Stay out of the way. This is
not the moment to tell him he's a drug abuser or an alcoholic. He
simply cannot understand. If your parent gets violent, phone 911.
In a quiet moment you may want to look for support groups
detailed in chapters 13 and 14 of this book.

When your parent is in the process of recovering, he will feel ill. If his moods have stabilized and if you can find it within your heart to show sympathy, then this may be the moment to talk to him. If you make accusations he will shut you out. Always use "I" statements and not accusations. You might tell him how worried, concerned, frightened, and helpless you felt while he was taking drugs or perhaps drinking.

My parents are divorced. My mother works in a department store. Almost every night she comes home smelling of alcohol and continues to drink all evening. When I mention the alcohol to her, she pretends she doesn't drink at home and says she only had one drink at work because she had to entertain an important customer. If I tell her I don't believe her, she tells me I am fresh. Is my mother an alcoholic?

Yes. Your mother's excuses as to "why I had to drink" are typical symptoms of the mental illness of addiction. Alcoholics are so afraid of what their drinking is doing to them, and their lack of control once they do drink, that they minimize the amount of alcohol they take and put the emphasis on why they had to drink. In a sense they are saying, "It is not my fault — politeness forced me to drink." So, you see, this is your mother's way of rationalizing her drinking to you and even more to herself. Your mother's need to be respected by you causes her to tell you that drinking is an important asset on her job. She is embarrassed that you know she is drinking.

I brought a friend home from school. The minute we walked into the house we could smell the sweet odor of marijuana. My mother offered us some chicken salad. She was so mellow that she talked slowly and kept stroking me. Finally she took the salad out of the refrigerator, scooped some of it with her fingers into her mouth, licked her fingers loudly, and kept putting the same fingers into the salad. I was so embarrassed that when my friend left I screamed at my mother, asking her why she had to smoke pot. My mother said it calmed her and told me to try some.

As you can see you should not try marijuana. Your mother is smoking pot to get a high. She may be suffering from depression. When she is not smoking, not high, you may want to tell her how you need a mother who is drug free. You may also want to speak to your school counselor and join a group such as Nar Anon, Alateen or Teen-Anon or any of the other groups mentioned in Chapter 14. It will change your life.

I brought a friend home from school. My mother offered to make us a peanut butter sandwich. She was so intoxicated that she spread the peanut butter on the table instead of on the bread. I felt so humiliated that when my friend left I burst out crying. In between sobs I kept asking my mother why she had to drink. My mother said she drinks because she needs a pick-me-up, feels depressed, and has many troubles and worries. I can't see what her worries are. My father supports us and is good to us. Are her feelings part of alcoholism?

Alcohol causes anxiety and depression. Many of your mother's emotional ups and downs would not be so great if she were able to give up alcohol. She uses her emotions as a reason for drinking. It is the drinking that is causing her extreme behavior. Once your mother realizes she is using alcohol as an erroneous cure for her intense emotions, and is able to examine these emotions, she may be able to accept alcoholism as an illness. In the meantime you may want to join Alateen. Once your mother notices that you are going for help she too may slowly realize that she has a disease.

I have recently started to date a girl who lives only a block from my house. She comes from what I think is a normal family. One evening I suggested we go to my house because I thought my father would be out. When we got to my house my father was there. He had some CDs on and was dancing faster than the music and every once in a while snorting cocaine. When he saw my girlfriend he grabbed her and said, "I'll show you how to dance." He was sweating, high, and acting edgy. My girlfriend ran out of the house. A few days later my father apologized to me and said it wouldn't happen again and that he really did not take drugs regularly. Is my father a drug addict?

Yes. No one should ever snort cocaine. Once the effects wear off, most people who take cocaine need more, feel sometimes paranoid, and will crave that high again. Your father needs treatment. His promises may be sincere, but he is denying the truth to himself–that he has a severe problem.

My father often gets intoxicated. Every time he gets drunk, he promises not to get drunk again. My father says any man who promises not to drink can stop drinking. Why hasn't he stopped drinking?

Your father's promises to stop drinking are one of the symptoms of alcoholism. When your father promises not to drink again, he honestly feels he can keep that promise. When your father takes that first drink, he feels that with a little discipline he can control the effects of alcohol on his behavior. Deep down he is frightened that he cannot. He is most likely wondering what has happened to him. He keeps asking himself if he is losing his mind. Until your father understands that alcoholism is an illness, he will feel bewildered and upset that he cannot control his drinking.

My father only drinks when something goes wrong at the office. Is that alcoholism too?

Anyone who drinks to solve a problem or because his day did not go right may become a substance abuser. However, it depends on how your father drinks. Does his drinking get out of control, or does he have only one or two drinks? Does he always drink when something goes wrong in his life, or only socially with your mother after a hard day's work? Review the eight statements listed earlier in this chapter to make sure you are not jumping to conclusions.

3

Blackouts, Unkept Promises, Unfair Criticism, and Family Arguments

WHY DO SOME **substance abusers make unrealistic promises when they take drugs?**

People on drugs are apt to make all kinds of promises to the family. They hope their promises will mask what they are doing and that drugs are more important to them than their families and life itself. The parent taking drugs may promise a new car, a much-wanted trip, a phone of your own in your room. The drug abuser hopes to gain the family's love and respect their deflated ego desperately craves. The drugs help the addicted parent feed his fantasy of what he would like to be able to do for his family and the kind of person he would like to be.

Why do some substance abusers while they are high criticize their children unfairly?

When a substance abuser criticizes or even insults the children unfairly, it is because the parent wants to be looked upon as a big, powerful, wonderful person and a successful parent.

Deep down, he hates himself and is suffering from this self-hate and guilt. To get relief, the abuser projects these self-critical feelings (such as "I am no good,"…"I am weak, a sissy") onto the nearest person. Remember, it may be feelings like these that trigger him to take drugs.

My mother is an alcoholic who never stops hurting our feelings. Is she aware she is insulting or making unrealistic promises to her family while under the influence of alcohol?

Most likely your parent, once she is sober, will not remember what she said or did. Alcohol is an anesthetic. When used over a long period of time, it can cause lapses of memory, known as blackouts.

Other parents, while not high on drugs but still feeling guilty and wanting to make up for the hurts they have caused also make unrealistic promises.

Can a parent's unfair criticism affect me?

If you have been subject to unfair criticism from birth it can discourage you from using your talents to the fullest, from completing chores and schoolwork. As an adult, it can even discourage you from going into a profession and keep you from a healthy loving relationship. This is why you need to get help. You can be taught to see yourself in your true light – as someone who can succeed.

Give an example of a teenager who became discouraged by unfair criticism from his parent.

Stuart is a typical sixteen-year-old boy who experienced and suffered from the criticism of an alcoholic parent. It seemed to Stuart the only thing his father ever had to say to him was, "You haven't got a brain in your head." Stuart was a sophomore in high school. It was true he was a poor student, or what his dean called an "underachiever." Even though Stuart knew he was an underachiever, he would have liked to hear his father say, just once, something else when he brought home his report card other than his usual, "You haven't got a brain in your head."

Stuart was determined to prove to his father that he did have a brain in his head. He studied very hard. Some nights it was difficult for him to concentrate on his homework because he could hear his parents bickering in the next room.

"You forgot to pay the mortgage again. The bank is fed up."

"How many times can a person smash up a car? I'm surprised they haven't taken your license away!"

"If you wouldn't drink so much…."

Stuart didn't like the bickering, and wondered if his parents might separate. He wondered, too, because his father was so forgetful about paying bills, if they might lose their home.

He kept telling himself that if he studied hard, maybe, by some miracle, things would get better at home.

Stuart's determination to concentrate on his schoolwork, in spite of the bickering and worries at home, paid off. His next report card showed a marked improvement. There was even a personal note of praise from his dean.

Proudly Stuart put the report card on his father's desk. Stuart felt happier than he had felt in a long time. He knew that his father could only be pleased with such a report, but more important, maybe now his father would realize that he was intelligent and would start paying some attention to him. Stuart could remember when his father used to go to ballgames and movies with him. Who knew? Maybe things would go back to the way they used to be. Stuart would offer to get a part-time job to help pay off some of the bills. He thought that might lessen some of the arguments at home and keep the family from breaking up. He would let his father know that he was old enough to understand things weren't always easy at the office.

When Stuart's father came home and saw the report, he said without hesitation, "Well, well, who did the work for you? I know you don't have the brains to do it!"

Stuart was stunned. All that work for nothing! He wouldn't be surprised if his father not only thought he was stupid but hated him, too.

Stuart would not have been as hurt if he had known his father was tied up in his own miserable feelings, which kept him from recognizing what Stuart had accomplished in school.

Do these parents who are substance abusers understand how they hurt their children?

Sometimes the parents do understand but do not know how to help themselves. Parents who are substance abusers are what they are because of their personality makeup and not because they want to hurt their children or be purposely unpleasant.

Where can one go when a parent is using drugs?

Go for a walk. Do your homework in the library. Visit a good friend, go to Alateen, a teenage walk-in center, community center, or get involved in after-school activities.

Develop options for your own safety and lifestyle.

Harold, who is married today and has children, told the following story about his youth. His mother was a marijuana abuser and his father was a heavy drinker. They both tended to get nasty when they were under the influence of their drugs. His parents' neighbors had children younger than Harold. Whenever something was wrong in his house Harold used to run next door. The neighbors took him in and included him around their dining table, in their outings and family festivities. In return Harold babysat for the family and refused to take money. Harold says that he learned to be a family man from his neighbors and not from his family.

My father smokes cocaine several days in a row. Should I stay away during these days?

Yes. Stay with a favorite aunt, cousin, or grandmother. Be sure that your mother knows where you are at all times. Your parent or the adult in charge of the substance abuser has enough problems without having to worry about where you might be. If you have no place to go and you feel you are in danger, call 911.

What can a teenager do if a drug-dependent parent becomes nasty and insulting?

The problem of living with a drug-dependent parent will become simplified if you can avoid a confrontation while your parent is abusing drugs. Detach yourself emotionally. Just keep telling yourself that your parent is ill and that her true self is not speaking to you. Not fighting back will conserve your strength for better things. If you must answer back, give an answer like, "I am your daughter (or son) and I love you." It may shock your parent into a moment of silence. The best thing to do when a parent is abusing drugs is to get out of the house.

If you feel physically threatened, dial 911.

How can we avoid repeating our families' mistakes?

Problems are a part of everyone's life, and the clue to coping with them is to understand ourselves and our environment. This means taking a close look at ourselves. It may be painful but it's worth it. It is important to recognize multigenerational patterns. Which of your own behavior is chosen, copied, or inherited? Only if we know why we act and feel the way we do will we be freed from repeating our families' mistakes. Seek out role models, other families you trust.

Keep in mind that when your parents were young they did not start out wanting to become addicts. One of your grandparents may have been an addict and your parents may have promised themselves that they would never use drugs or alcohol like someone in their family did. Whatever your parents (or parent) experimented with they felt they would stay in control. They would be different than other addicts.

Remember, your parents' drinking and drugging started out "just for fun." These diseases are progressive however, and you, as their teenagers, are seeing them when they are unable to stop without help.

We may innocently try a cigarette out of curiosity or to feel adult, without realizing that nicotine is a gateway drug that can be the first in a succession of substance abuse. We know this from statistics, which show that people who don't smoke have a lower rate of drinking problems and other drug use.

Similarly we may decide to have just one beer to feel at one with a crowd. Well, why not have another one? And so it begins.

The safest course is not to experiment with any drugs, including alcohol and cigarettes. A lot has to do with your view of life, what you want for yourself and what friends you choose.

Is it true that some drug abusers are very quiet while using a drug, and it is their children who start to fight with the drug abuser?

Sometimes youngsters are so angry at their parent's taking drugs or drinking that they pick a fight to "get back at him." It makes these youngsters angry that their parent cannot be responsive when they need him to give the parental attention they want and deserve.

Should one stay away from every discussion with the drug abuser — even when she is not taking drugs?

When your parent is not taking drugs, not drinking, listen to her. You may find that she has some good things to say. Children who have a substance abuser in their midst have to learn to tell the difference between sober discussions, thoughtful adult criticism, and those arguments caused by the substance.

What are sober arguments, sober criticism, and sober discussion?

Sober arguments, as referred to in this book, are those discussions in a family that are caused not by substance abuse but by normal day-to-day life. For instance, if the drug-dependent parent complains that his son or daughter stays out too late at night, he may have a valid concern that has nothing to do with his substance abuse.

In some families the children are so used to ignoring the drug-dependent parent that they might be tempted to dismiss the drug-dependent's concern with a "but you smoke pot regularly" or "but you drink" retort. It is unfair to the drug abuser and a good way to avoid an important but inconvenient subject.

Don't forget that a parent may be abusing drugs to escape unpleasant feelings about himself. If you can, when the drug-dependent parent is sober, make him feel an important part of the family. This may motivate him to learn about his illness.

My mother loses her temper when my father drinks. I don't blame my mother, and I take her side. My father gets furious with me for what he calls interfering. Wouldn't you think, as a daughter, I have the right to interfere?

We are often tempted to take sides when parents argue. Parents argue because they have reached the limit of their patience. When you take sides, it gives them more reasons to argue, and one parent may feel that you are teaming up against him or her. Teenagers usually take the side of the parent who they feel protects them and who they feel may be threatened. Before getting involved in your parents' argument, decide what can be accomplished by interfering. Too often, such interference may lead to further isolation from one parent.

Both my parents are alcoholics. When they argue, they ask me for my opinion. Consequently, without wanting to, I get involved in their arguments. How can I get them to leave me alone?

Answer them honestly. "I would like to help you, but I don't know how." If that does not work, go for a walk.

4

Drug Dependencies and Your Parent's Job

I AM AFRAID my father will lose his job because of his drugging. How can we help him hide his problem in the hope that his company won't notice it?

Very often, out of fear that the substance abuser may lose his job, the family will help him hide his drugging from the world. If he has a hangover, the family may think they are helping him out by calling his company and saying he won't be in because he has a "cold" or a "virus." An employer soon sees through such excuses.

When a family makes excuses for the substance abuser, they are in a sense allowing the illness to progress. Deep down, the substance abuser feels he can continue his drugging because the family will help by covering up for him. The family is hiding his addiction as a disgrace instead of openly declaring it as a problem that can be treated.

When a company recognizes it has a drugging employee, is it likely that the substance abuser will eventually lose his job?

Not necessarily. Some companies have excellent programs to help the substance abuser. Rather than fire the substance abuser, the medical department, the personnel department, or the boss will inform the substance abuser that the deterioration in his work has been noticed. A medical check-up or professional counseling may be suggested. The doctor will question the parent about his habits and explain what resources the company or community offers.

Very often a boss can get the substance abuser to accept the problem more readily than the family can. Deep down, he is afraid of losing her job. When a boss speaks to the substance abuser, he can no longer fool himself, and this may motivate him to seek professional help.

My father is an alcoholic. In that case, isn't it fair to tell my father's company that he drinks?

Definitely not. Your father's drinking is an illness, and he has to take the steps to help himself. Your best course of action is not to interfere.

My father smokes crack. What will happen to our family if he should lose his job?

Financial problems can become serious for the family. It may be necessary to seek outside help. While this is not pleasant to think about, it is also true that such a situation may shock the substance abuser into realizing that he is ill and must have help to deal with his illness.

My father is a heroin addict who lost his job due to his habit. My mother has taken a job. My father has still not given up using heroin or sought help. What can we do?

Your family can do a lot to help your father. Your father is, most likely, unhappy that he has lost his job. He may rationalize that it wasn't his drug habit that cost him his job, but something else, such as a lack of ability. He can use such illusions as an excuse to continue using heroin. The family should try to tell your father how his habit is hurting the family, how they miss having a father. He should be told that he is capable of gaining his health back. Once your father sees his situation in the proper light, he may seek out a clinic, a hospital, or other facilities that offer help and hope for recovery. You can also try intervention, which is explained in great detail in Chapter 10.

My mother is an illustrator of children's books. After she finishes a project she always drinks too much. Why is that?

Like other substance abusers, the alcoholic drinks to suppress emotional discomfort. Your mother may be a perfectionist who feels inadequate about even her best work as an artist. Some substance abusers rationalize that their finished piece of work deserves a celebration and reward themselves by going on a binge. Or it is possible that your mother feels insufficient as a human being and that these feelings were temporarily repressed during the period of artistic creativity. Many successful people have become alcoholics for similar reasons. Did you know, for example, that such famous writers as O. Henry, Stephen Crane, Sinclair Lewis, F. Scott Fitzgerald, Edgar Allan Poe, and Eugene O'Neill were all alcoholics?

5

Problems Faced by Your Sober Parent

DOES EVERY PARENT who lives with a drug abuser suffer from strain and tension?

Yes. Any parent who lives with a drug abuser has many emotional burdens and much pressure to bear.

What are some of these pressures and emotional burdens?

The parent who lives with a drug abuser is continually nagged by worry. How can he protect the children from the parent abusing drugs? The sober parent has to make decisions alone regarding their children and wonders what the drug abuse will do to the family's economic status. He may wonder if the children will be able to finish school or if the family will have to move.

The sober parent has to face the loss of friends who do not want to deal with the ups and downs of a drug abuser. The sober parent has to try to explain to relatives, who know nothing about addiction, what has happened in their home. The sober parent lacks companionship in the evening and has to take over chores that the drug abuser would normally undertake. The parent living with a drug abuser can never plan anything confidently.

My mother's live-in boyfriend is a substance abuser. My mother seems perfectly relaxed to me.

Your mother may act with sureness and capability on the surface, as an attempt to protect you and to keep your home together. But, deep down, she is anxious about all she has to take care of. You should try to live with another relative or a friend while your mother is living with a substance abuser. You may want to discuss this situation with a school counselor and get in touch with Alateen and the other resources listed at the end of this book.

Can all these emotions complicate the relationship between the sober parent and the children?

Yes. In many cases, parents who live with extreme anxiety caused by addiction cannot express their true thoughts. In some instances, yelling at the nearest member of the family becomes an outlet for pent up feelings. Deep down they are ashamed of themselves for yelling and are wondering what is happening to them. There are times when the sober parent worries if she, too, is becoming ill.

My mother, who is an alcoholic, will put up with anything we want. My father, who is not an alcoholic, is always in a bad mood. He says my mother spoils us. Why can't my father take things a little more easy?

What your father is trying to tell you is that, while your mother permits you to do anything to gain your love, he is left with the unpleasant task of saying no when the need arises. This does not always endear him to you. When your father does not get the cooperation and the understanding he deserves for his decisions and actions, he may become ill tempered.

Remember, too, that your father may be extra tense if he has to go to work and leave the house in the charge of your alcoholic mother. He knows that his children may come home from school to a locked door and that your alcoholic mother may be lying unconscious within the house. He knows that you may be ashamed to bring home friends because of your mother's behavior. He worries whether the refrigerator will be empty at dinnertime because the household money was spent on liquor. You can ease the tension at home by trying to understand your father's position and offering to cooperate with him in every way possible.

My father smokes cocaine and can't hold a job. My mother is now supporting us. We thought once Mom had a steady job our lives would be easier. Why have our lives become more complicated instead, and why do we argue more than ever before?

In any home, any illness, not just substance abuse, can upset interfamily relationships because the roles get shifted around. The older son may, for instance, have to give up a club meeting or a ball game to take care of the younger children. Your mother can't drive you to the pool or to a friend's house because she has to go to work. Of course, substance abuse puts the whole house in danger. You don't know how your parent will act out. Will he become violent? Will you have to phone 911?

Conversely, if a mother is the substance abuser, a father can't relax on the weekends with his children because he has extra responsibilities.

The family has to recognize that money for a second family car, a vacation, or an evening out may be spent on medical care.

Unless the family understands the situation, the pressure can cause almost unbearable emotional chaos. Your best course of action is to sit down as a family and make a schedule of your chores, including your parent who works.

My mother has left my father because he started to smoke crack. She works and I try to help her. But she is unreasonable. If I am out playing baseball with the guys, she'll call me off a base just to put the laundry in the dryer. Is this type of behavior fair?

No, it is not fair. Your mother acts this way because she is so tired that it's hard for her to get up from her chair to put the laundry in the dryer. A contributing factor to your mother's tiredness is the fact that she has suppressed her problems while on the job all day. She cannot discuss with everyone her many worries and her loneliness. A simple, straightforward reply to your mother's unexpected requests may avert an argument. Try saying, "May I do it as soon as I come in? I joined this game before I knew you had a chore for me." You'll discover if you really do the chore later, your mother will be more likely to trust you to schedule your own work.

I understand that my mother has to work and may be tired. Sometimes when I stay around the house to help. she will explode and shout, "Get out of the house, go visit your friends!" How am I to know what to do?

Teenagers who live in a home where there is substance abuse complain frequently about one of the parents exploding for no reason in particular. When we live with tension, we become explosive. Since most of us would be embarrassed to burst out in public, we let it out mostly on those we love.

While your mother does sound harsh, all she is saying is, "I had a hard day at the office. Conferences, constant chatter, computer problems. I can't take anymore, not even affection." This does not mean that you should really get out of the house as your mother requested. If you stay, you may find what your mother really wants is someone to talk to.

My mother is an alcoholic. I am a sixteen-year-old girl and my father worries about me unduly. If I go to a girlfriend's house, he worries if I will be safe, if it is safe for me to walk home alone, and if I will have a drink while I am out. Why does my father worry more than other fathers do?

Your father worries because the daughter of an alcoholic mother is at risk of also becoming an alcoholic. Because alcoholism is an addiction that is hereditary, your father knows you should not even experiment or try alcohol. Furthermore your are not yet of legal age and as the sober parent he feels responsible for you.

In the meantime, you can reassure your father by being supportive. Let your father know that you do not drink, where you are going, what you are doing. Phone him if you are going to be late. If he expresses a fear, talk it over with him even if it is a far-fetched fear. You might even try signing a "contract" with your father spelling out that you will not experiment with drugs or alcohol and other details that worry him.

6

Let's Take a Good Look at Ourselves

MY MOTHER IS an alcoholic. I am so frightened when she drinks that there are times when I can't sleep, and I can't concentrate in school. What can I do to calm myself?

The constant fear that comes from living with an alcoholic or any substance-abusing parent can exhaust and wear all family members down. This is why addiction is called the "family disease."

You will find your difficulties less scary if you have an objective person to talk to. All members of a family who have an alcoholic in their midst should never hesitate to talk to their school counselor, clergyperson, an Alcoholics Anonymous member, to someone from Al-Anon or Alateen, or to their family doctor. These people have experience in helping you to learn how to deal with alcoholism and to sort out those worries you can solve and those you should leave to your parents. While A.A., Al-Anon and Alateen help those with alcoholism and cross addictions there are also Nar Anon Family Groups and Narcotics Anonymous, which help those families coping with other drug addictions.

My parent is in a rehabilitation center for drug-dependent people. I am in a therapy group for teenagers who live with drug-dependent parents. I noticed that a lot of the kids in my group said that they feel as if their drug-dependent parents don't care for them at all—especially while that parent is smoking pot, taking pills, drinking, or snorting crack. I agree with them. If my parent loved me she would not have taken all those pills.

In part you feel this way because you are projecting your wish that your parent had never become addicted to those pills. Until a teenager accepts the fact that her parent has an illness, that teenager is going to say, "If my parent loved me she wouldn't swallow those pills."

Another reason you feel "unloved" by your parent is because of the inconsistency in your home. This inconsistency is one of the biggest problems a teenager has when living with a drug-dependent parent. The effects of drug dependency cause the parent to show too much love one day and too little the next. One day your parent may praise you and the next day embarrass you. One day the substance abuser may sleep all day and the next day need all your attention. Under such conditions, it is very hard for the abuser to consistently show real parental feelings.

Emotional inconsistency is part of the pattern of all drug-dependent parents.

My mother is an alcoholic. My sister is on hard drugs. Can alcoholism in our home have driven her to taking drugs?

Studies have shown that there are more drug users among the children of alcoholic parents. Your sister is in a sense copying your mother by using a chemical stimulus to satisfy her needs and, like your mother, she is attempting to get satisfaction from sources other than real life. Knowing all this may not help you too much in solving your family's problems. You should see them as individual cases and help them as such. Most of all, don't assign automatic blame to your mother for your sister's problem. Try to find a drug-help center in your town and ask them what steps you should take to help your sister. Get help for yourself. Join Alateen, Family Anonymous, and the other organizations listed at the end of this book. A counselor may help you to do an intervention with your sister and /or your mother. You should never attempt to organize an intervention without proper support from a counselor or a rehabilitation center. Intervention is explained in detail in Chapter 10.

I have heard it said that sometimes a teenager feels guilty because one of his parents is a drug abuser. Why should a teenager feel guilty if his parent takes pills, drinks, or snorts cocaine?

A teenager who lives with a drug abuser should not feel guilty because of his parent's habits. Sometimes teenagers in this situation may wonder if their behavior and their relationship with that parent may be driving him to abuse drugs.

Every family has problems and differences. A son or daughter may be dating someone whom his or her parents do not approve of. A teenager may have taken up a lifestyle that goes against the family traditions. The teenager may mistakenly think these problems are driving the parent to drugs. But it is not the problems and differences within the family that are driving the parent to take drugs. It is the drug habit itself that has weakened his or her parent's ability to handle day-to-day family stress.

Couldn't some of these problems and emotions, such as not feeling loved, feeling guilty and nervous, occur in non-drug abusing families too?

Absolutely. Drug abusers are by no means the only people with problems. Extreme poverty, a father who works too hard and ignores the family, a mother who prefers the Internet to her children, or any other serious kind of personality conflicts within the family may easily cause problems.

If you feel you do have a problem, whatever your problem may stem from — it pays to make the effort to deal with that problem while you are still young.

What is most important in family life?

A family exists to help its members. A family should provide an atmosphere where each individual can mature and thrive. A family should be a foundation from which a teenager can test himself and grow in the outside world.

Are drug-dependent parents at all interested in hearing how their children feel about family problems?

Many teenagers avoid discussion with their parents, even when the drug-dependent parent is not taking drugs, because they are afraid of a difference of opinion. If you talk sensibly about how you feel about your family, sticking to facts rather than criticizing, your parents might appreciate your feelings.

On the other hand you must remember that just because someone has stopped drinking or taking drugs it does not mean that she has healed her mind and spirit. You know your parent best. You might consider having another adult whom you trust present when you discuss anything serious with your parent.

7

Your Responsibility to Yourself and to Your Family

MY MOTHER IS an alcoholic. We don't have a father. I am the eldest of three children. Every time my mother passes out, I have to cancel dates and miss school because I end up not only nursing her but also taking care of my brother and sister. What can I do to help myself in a situation like this?

Every time your mother passes out you need to call 911. Such a condition may be life threatening.

While your mother is incapacitated, you should do as few of her chores as possible. If you stay home from school to take over her job, you will be allowing her to continue this pattern. This is called "enabling." If your mother works outside the home, she may ask you to call the office for her when she doesn't feel well. By insisting that she herself do this, you may help her to see her problem from a different perspective.

Many a mother has pulled herself together because her family or younger child needed her. If a mother is made to feel that her chores, her way of parenting, even her cooking can be replaced, she will continue to drink. When your mother is sober, you should tell her what it is like for you when she drinks, without criticizing or insulting her. She may never have thought about what it is like for a son or daughter to stay home from school, or have to cope with a mother's household chores. She may not know that you miss her when she passes out.

Do not hesitate to go for help to any of the teen groups listed at the end of this book. Seek advice from family service, a school counselor, or a teenage walk-in center.

Whenever my mother is not taking her pills, she expects my brother and me to do all the cleaning. If we do not do a good job, she hits us. What can we do to make her stop being so finicky?

No parent should physically or verbally abuse a child. Your mother may be a perfectionist who is, when not taking her pills, projecting her frustrated, unhappy, miserable feelings onto you.

Is it at all possible for you to talk to your mother and make her aware that because of school you can devote only one or two hours a day to housework? Frequently, the only solution is a schedule. This weekly schedule might include everything from "study for history exam" to "drama club" or "swim at the Y." You may even suggest signing a contract with your mother as to what you should do in the house.

You may find that once your mother knows you are not wasting time while not doing the housework, she will become more tolerant toward your work. Should your mother not be receptive to your needs, then her problem is one you cannot be expected to cope with. Many teenagers suffer from physical abuse by a parent or parents. You should seek help from a family service, a teenage walk-in center, or your clergyperson.

Both my parents are substance abusers who are now in AA and family counseling. This counselor who has been working with us has told me I should help my parents in the house. I don't know why but my father tends to throw up. He also loses his temper and throws things around. What is the use of straightening up the house if one of my parents throws up and messes everything up again?

As a member of the household you have responsibilities, but it is not your job to clean up after your substance-abusing parent. You should ask to speak to the family counselor or tell your story at an Alateen meeting.

Should a substance abuser mess up the house after you cleaned it, it is very understandable that you would be most annoyed. However, once you decide to straighten up the house, do not use as an excuse "maybe my father will go wild again." Simple everyday attitudes, like finishing what we start, get us into good work habits for the time we will be living on our own and holding down a job.

My father died when I was six years old and my mother remarried quickly. My mother and stepfather are both heavy marijuana smokers. When my stepfather smokes he makes sexual demands on me. When I complain to my mother, she slaps me and says I am imagining the whole thing. What can I do?

Nobody has the right to make sexual demands on you. You need to protect yourself. It is important that you immediately seek professional help. Your school nurse, physician, school counselor, children services, your local mental health clinic or family counseling service, and hotlines should all be able to aid you. Should you not feel comfortable with the first person you approach, then seek someone else to talk to. The goal is to find someone who will not only believe you and understand the terror, but also aid you in rebuilding your life. By law, whoever you talk to has to report the sexual abuse. If no one is there to help you when your stepfather approaches you, you can dial 911.

You might like to know that most agencies today encourage family counseling as well as marital and individual counseling. The intent is to rebuild the family and avoid any loss of jobs and standing in the community. During this healing period, while you work out what has happened, your stepfather may be asked to leave the family.

Your mother and stepfather probably as children had poor parenting and, in a sense, are still like children today. Of course drug abuse complicates all problems. Often the victim is made to feel guilty. Such comments as "you're imagining it" or "you asked for it" or "if you tell anyone you will be in big trouble" are all guilt trips to keep you quiet. You are innocent and should not feel guilty.

The main point is that you get help. You should not need to deal with this yourself.

My mother likes martinis, takes pills, and smokes marijuana. I work very hard at home trying to help. I think one of the reasons I work so hard is that I want to be appreciated. But I do not get any consideration from my family. How can I get my family to appreciate me more?

First of all something should be done to get your mother off drugs. Is your father around or some other relative who can help? You should speak to your school counselor.

Try to spend time with those who appreciate you - friends, cousins, a teacher, and clubs and organizations like Alateen.

Your mother's addiction makes her extremely self-centered. She is protecting her right to drink and smoke. Even when she will be sober it will take her time to understand the needs of others.

Whenever I mention my problems to my friends' parents they say go to your school counselor. I don't think much of my school counselor. The kids in school say the counselor herself drinks heavily on weekends. What can I do? Where can a thirteen-year-old go for help?

Much depends on the size of your community and the services available. Is there a Nar Anon Family Group, Al-Anon, Alateen, or an Alcoholics Anonymous near you where some of the older members can help you? Do you have access to the Internet where you can seek out an organization such as listed at the end of this book? The important thing is not to give up and to seek out others in a similar situation. The home offices of Nar Anon Family Groups, Alateen, and Alcoholics Anonymous, all listed at the end of this book, will help you start a group in your hometown.

My father is in prison for possession of cocaine with the intent to sell. I know that my father only sold cocaine so that he would have the money to smoke it. He called it his pocket money. I love my father and miss him. I am afraid that we will lose touch permanently. What can I do?

Write letters and notes to your father. Tell him about school, what courses you are taking, what sports you are doing, who you are seeing. Enclose cartoons, jokes you have heard and photos of you and your family. Let him know that you want to hear from him.

Sometimes prison has a positive effect. Many addicts get over their addiction in prison — especially if there is a treatment program in the facility. You may find it beneficial to attend some of the teen groups listed at the end of this book so that you may find other teenagers who have had a parent in prison and may now be back home.

My father came out of prison clean, but he is not pleasant. What can I do to make our home life more bearable?

You father needs to continue with his sobriety program. Your father probably took drugs or alcohol because he was an unhappy person to begin with, and he may still be unhappy. He needs to join Narcotics Anonymous or Alcoholics Anonymous. Be careful what you say to your father. You do not want to tell him what to do. What you can do is join one of the groups mentioned at the end of this book. You will meet other youngster in the same position. When your father notices that you are seeking help he too may want to join a group.

I am in a foster home because both my parents smoke pot. How can I convince the social agency to let me live with my parents?

You might ask your social worker if you could visit your parents one afternoon a week. If your social worker feels this might not be good for you or your parents who are trying to heal you can still write them. Tell them what you are doing, about your home and tell them that you look forward to seeing them soon. Let your social worker know that you want to join a teen self-help group so that you can meet with teens in similar situations.

Michael who attended such a group told the following story. "I was not happy to live in a foster home. Fortunately I had a nice social worker who visited me about once a month. As I told her what I did not like about my foster parents she made me aware that I was really annoyed that my real parents couldn't provide a home for me and I was taking it out on my foster parents. She called it displaced anger. My parents never became clean, but my foster family and I became friends. I am eighteen now and have been accepted by our local community college. I have a part time job and as I continue school I plan to keep on living with my foster family. Because I am of legal age I'll be paying them rent."

8

It's Your School Life and Future

MY MOTHER IS in treatment for taking methamphetamine. She exhausts me and keeps me from studying. What can I do?

First of all, join Nar Anon. There you will find teenagers who face similar problems. You will be able to share your feelings and make new friends. Try to get your father (or if you have no father, a professional person) to take an interest in your problem. Your father may never have realized that your mother is so demanding and noisy when you are with her that you cannot get your homework done. He may not know that, because she is a substance abuser, she has forgotten notices, meetings, and conferences with your school or has embarrassed you socially in school.

Your father may never have been aware that your mother, like so many substance abusers, may criticize whatever you do so much that she may have undermined your self-confidence and capability to do schoolwork.

You should plan to do your homework outside your home. Is there a library nearby? A friend who has a home where you could study? Could you ask to go to boarding school, or if your family can't afford a boarding school, could you apply for a scholarship?

How can students who do poorly in school because of the substance abuse in the home help themselves?

In the files of a public school counselor is the case history of Kenneth, a boy who was determined to do something about his predicament.

Fifteen-year-old Kenneth knew that he wanted to be a carpenter. He had looked into the requirements and realized that he would need special training. Kenneth was doing so badly in school that he was seriously thinking of dropping out; but first, he decided, he would discuss it with his school counselor. The counselor arranged to have Kenneth tested. Kenneth showed good ability in his tests. Upon further questioning, the counselor learned that Kenneth had trouble concentrating because he felt worried and was restless and tired most of the time. The counselor questioned Kenneth about his study schedule at home. Kenneth explained that he could not keep a study schedule. His mother was an alcoholic. His father traveled a lot, so she drank mostly in the evening when she was alone.

Kenneth usually went to bed at eleven. His mother would come and wake him at one in the morning, not realizing the time, and say, "I am lonely, why don't you talk to me?" His mother had been placed in a hospital several times. It always upset Kenneth to see the ambulance arrive. While his mother was in the hospital, he had to do many time-consuming chores that left him too tired for his homework. Kenneth concluded, "Counseling can't change my home life, and how your testing can help someone like me is beyond me."

The counselor had Kenneth's father come to school to see what arrangements could be made for Kenneth to sleep at a friend's house whenever his mother drank. She also encouraged his father to attend Alanon meetings and Kenneth to go to Alateen.

What interested the counselor was that Kenneth told her he could not concentrate even when he tried to study in school, at a friend's house, or at the library. The counselor told Kenneth that it was understandable a life such as his would make a teenager angry and keep him from studying. She went on to tell him that this type of anger may frequently be against oneself, and it might, in part, be anger that has nothing to do with the family.

Any teenager may be upset that he does not achieve his high expectations in school. This may include not only grades but also popularity, athletic achievements, and coping with personal problems. The pretty girl in algebra class does not even know you are alive. Or, that handsome boy in intermediate Spanish does not even nod at you.

Kenneth asked, "But what about the feeling of frustration and anger that you can't pinpoint?" He said this was how he felt different from the other students. He could understand why he was upset when his social life was bad or his mother drank; but he also said he had this upset feeling even when his mother was not drinking, and all was well in school. His mind would wander to the last time his mother drank, or he would worry if she might drink again. Then one day, while discussing this feeling with his counselor, he made an admission to himself that opened a whole new outlook on the problem. Kenneth, because he loved his parents, wanted things to be right at home. Since he could not make them right, he felt frustrated and angry with himself. This was, in part, why he could not concentrate. Once he understood where his restlessness came from, he had a certain amount of relief.

The counselor told Kenneth many teenagers from nonalcoholic homes feel a similar restlessness. There are teenagers whose parents want to get divorced, or who have a parent in debt or continually in court. They feel frustrated, too, that they cannot solve their parents' problems. Unfortunately, there are some problems that never can be solved, and it is a waste of energy to worry over them. The only thing a teenager can do is recognize those problems that do not belong to him and try not to worry about them.

It is a big and difficult job, but it can be achieved. At first Kenneth thought he could never do it. But he found the more he practiced it, the more it helped him.

Alateen opens all meetings with this prayer:

> God grant me the serenity
> To accept the things I cannot change,
> Courage to change the things I can,
> And wisdom to know the difference.

Kenneth might encourage his mother not to drink by letting her know that chronic drinking is a disease, but he could not solve her drinking problem for her. Nor would it help him or his mother to worry about when she might have to go to the hospital.

Worrying can be a form of procrastination. You sit down to study, but you let your mind dwell on other things: "If Mom didn't drink, we would have a less banged-up home." Yet when you go to an interesting movie, your mind does not wander because you want to enjoy yourself.

Kenneth's counselor told him that when he found it hard to concentrate, he should phone a friend he could trust and talk out his feelings. Talking about frustrations and fears helps to overcome helpless and angry feelings. This is why talking out your feelings with a trusted person is so helpful.

Kenneth also made new friends at Alateen who let him sleep at their house whenever his mother drank so that Kenneth got plenty of sleep and could do his homework in peace.

Do all children of substance abusers have problems in school?

No. As contradictory as it may seem, many students who have drug-dependent parents, because of what they have experienced at home, are often more self-sufficient and stand up better to the challenge in school than their colleagues. Because a substance-abusing parent is a demanding parent, his son or daughter frequently turns out to be an above-average student.

How can my going to a counselor or joining a self-help group make life better at home when my parent is drugging and drinking?

Even if your parent continues drinking or taking drugs, at least you will learn how not to let their addiction manipulate and control you. You will learn how not to be an enabler. You will see that your parent's addiction is not your responsibility, nor need you be embarrassed by your parent's inappropriate behavior. It is not your doing.

Very often when a drugging or drinking parent sees a child take action to recover control of his life, make plans for a future, he will often seek help himself. The important thing is that someone in the family is getting better.

What is an enabler?

An enabler is the person who (often without realizing it) helps the addict to continue drinking or drugging. For example, if an alcoholic has a hangover, someone in the family may call his office and say he has a cold rather than let the alcoholic face his own problems. Or, if a parent is sick because he has been drugging, you take care of him—give him tea in bed, cook him a meal, or change his sheets.

9

Friends and Dating

SHOULD I TELL MY **friends my mother is a substance abuser before I bring them home?**

If you are truly embarrassed by your mother's drugging or drinking, maybe you should phone home before you bring a friend over. If your mother sounds bad on the phone, and you do not choose to tell your friends about the drugging or drinking at home, you can explain to your friend that your mother is sick today.

Many teenagers today want to confide in their friends. They say it is easier today than ever before to explain their parents' addictions to other teenagers because television, the movies, and magazines have publicized this disease.

Other teenagers of drinking or drugging parents feel they can bring their friends home without any explanations. It does not matter to them if their friends see their parents out of sorts once in a while. They feel it is not necessary to share the information that they live with drugging or drinking parents. The friend's natural reaction will probably be that it happens only occasionally.

Most of these boys and girls generally think that if their friends in school have not had experience with substance abuse, and they start to tell them about it, their friends will not know how to handle the information. While meaning well, friends might come up to them frequently and ask, "How are things at home?" as if he or she expected a sob story from them every other day.

My father is an alcoholic. One night I had a rough time at home. Foolishly I confided my problems to one of the boys in school who promptly burst out laughing and yelled, "Oh, boy, your old man gets stoned!" What can make a teenager act so unkindly?

People sometimes react with laughter when they don't know how to handle a situation or when they are presented with familiar facts in an unfamiliar environment. Most youngsters giggle at anything unfamiliar, such as the idea of an intoxicated parent, when they are ten, eleven, or twelve. You should remind your friends that substance abuse is a physical disease and it is not a question of a healthy person acting bad. The older we get, the better we accept unfamiliar facts. By the time we are thirteen or fourteen, we are capable of "putting our feet in someone else's shoes."

Only an insecure thirteen or fourteen year old teenager would be prompted to make an unkind remark. Making fun of someone else makes the insecure person feel as if he or she is super OK.

A helpful guideline is to remember that when we are upset we cannot explain things very well. This is the time we want to confide in a true and trustworthy friend — or in someone who has a similar situation at home.

I have a few good friends who have no experience with substance abuse. I feel guilty when I explain to them the situation at home. How can I confide in my close friends?

As long as you explain your parent's condition as an illness, but do not get personal about their actions (such as how they walk or talk), there is no reason to feel guilty about what you confide in a friend.

My mother is alcoholic. I can remember when, as a little kid, mothers didn't let their children play at my house because they didn't trust my home. Today, I am the one who is too embarrassed to let the kids see what state my mother is in. How can I ever make friends?

The opportunities for teenagers of alcoholic or drugging parents to meet new people are no different from those for any other teenager. When you were little you met children at the playground or in front of the house where the other mothers could see and supervise what was going on. But today you are a teenager, and as a teenager your opportunities to meet friends are almost all outside your home. You meet people in school, clubs, churches, syna-gogues, or where you have a job. When you meet someone for the first time in school, at that moment, the boy or girl you are talking to cannot see your father, mother, sister, brother, or your furniture, or your house. By the time you bring your friend home, the impression of you will already be formed. In your mind, as you talk to a fellow teenager, you may think of your home environment and feel awkward and uncomfortable. Our frame of mind can often keep us from acting like the warm and considerate persons we really are. You may feel uncomfortable because you remember when, as a young child, mothers did not want their children to play with you. This experience is over and should not stop you from making friends today.

The type of parents you have does not solely determine your popularity. There are plenty of youngsters who have pleasant par-ents but are unpopular because they are shy, insecure, or hesitant in reaching for others. A likable person is someone who is sincere, has unique ideas, is considerate, and is unselfish.

Isn't it true that it is hard to have really close friends if you cannot bring a friend home?

Good friends will understand the situation in your house and why you don't bring them to your home. They themselves may not want to go to your home when your parent is drugging or drinking. This is no reason to break up good friendships. You can reciprocate any friend's hospitality in other ways, such as helping him or her to get chores done quickly, helping with the dishes if you are invited for a meal, and just by being a sincere friend.

Remember, your friends probably want friends as much as you do.

My father is a substance abuser who has stopped taking pills. He is still very rigid and tense. The slightest noise upsets him. I literally cannot bring friends home. I would like to give a party at my house. How can I get my father to change?

With participation in Narcotics Anonymous, your father will find help and support. He will probably need to make big changes in his life to relax and enjoy his drug-free life.

You may have fun outside the home by going bowling or skating with your friends. Or perhaps you are lucky enough to have a relative or a good friend who would let you give a party in their home. People who offer their home should be given the following courtesy:

1. Assure your hosts that your friends will not use and do not ever use drugs or alcohol.

2. Ask your hosts how many people you may invite. Every homeowner knows, from past experience how many people are comfortable in his home.

3. Discuss in great detail what kind of party it will be — a barbecue, dancing, etc. This way your hosts will not surprise you the night of the party by saying, "All those CDs? We

thought you were just going to have one guitar. The neighbors will never stand for all that noise."

4. Ask your hosts whether they or someone else will be home the night of the party. After all, it is not your home, and if something goes wrong, you are better off having an adult around to take responsibility. An adult can handle anyone trying to crash your party or any impulsive guests.

5. Offer to pay for the refreshments.

6. Offer to clean up after the party.

The next day phone or write a thank you note. It might be a nice gesture to buy a little gift to thank them for the use of their home.

I know of a teenager whose birthday is in the summer. He has a barbecue every summer at a lakeside beach. His friends are so used to having this party that they by now ask him what should they bring—the Cokes? the hamburger rolls? One of the mothers is so impressed she always bakes a cake.

My father disapproves of the gang I hang around with. I disapprove of his smoking. Do I have a right to tell him to mind his own business?

Even though your father is a substance abuser, he is your parent and does worry about you. Among other things, he is worried you may end up like him—a substance abuser. Remember, your father probably started smoking thinking that it was a harmless habit and he could quit any time. He is worried you might do drugs.

Parents worry about gangs because who you select as friends can mean life or death. If your crowd believes in antisocial acts such as fast driving or stealing, or going to parties where drugs are used, even though you might not join in these activities, you could make yourself look guilty.

Teenagers who feel they want popularity will sometimes join a crowd. There is a form of security in a gang. In a gang, teenagers feel they belong. There is a leader to follow. Members will let all joiners feel they are welcome if the teenagers do what they want. Those who do not comply are left out. Before you join the gang, have a look at whether they're doing your type of thing. Those who look for nothing but a gang of friends are apt to have very few friends. They are so busy getting to know everyone that they have no time to get to know a few people well. If you are having problems breaking away from a gang, or have difficulty making friends on your own, join organized sports, a club at your local church, or group activities at your YMCA, YWCA, or your community center.

Perhaps substance abuse in the home can make a person too sensitive. I personally find that my feelings are easily hurt. What can I do to help myself?

The very experience of growing up, the hormonal changes in the body, and newly awakened interest in the opposite sex can make any teenager feel sensitive.

Naturally, any extreme problem, such as substance abuse, can make us even more sensitive and vulnerable. Should your drugging parent be the same sex as you, it is doubly difficult for you to find an image you can believe in and a role model to make you feel secure. Once you are aware of your need to have an image of your parent to be proud of, you can try to take those values you admire when your parent is sober. Should your parent's drugging have turned you off to such a degree that you cannot be objective even when she is sober, then seek out a counselor of your own sex to discuss your feelings. Many teenagers choose a model other than their parent.

My father is a substance abuser and always interferes with my dating. The trouble is that his rules for dating vary from day to day. What can I do?

If your parent is under the influence of drugs, try to set sensible and consistent dating standards for yourself. Should you not be able to get the kind of information you want from your family, pick out a family you admire and ask the teenager in that family about the standards or rules for dating. Or, if you do not know such a family, do not hesitate to discuss your dating with a counselor at a teenage walk-in center, at a teen Internet portal, or with a favorite clergyperson.

Some parents, even when they are sober, have a hard time setting rules and make different rules every time their son or daughter goes out. When your parent is sober, if he is willing, try signing a contract with him. The contract might include what time you need to be home, where you may and may not go, abstinence from alcohol and drugs, and safe sexual behavior or abstinence.

You may find that on the day that your father insists you "be home by 10 o'clock," something prompted him to be fearful. It may have been an article he read in the newspaper about a teenager getting killed in a car accident. You might, in fact, ask him why he wants you home earlier this time. His explanation may be reasonable. Whatever the reason, and no matter how unpleasantly he expresses it, he is showing concern for you.

The main principle here is that you distinguish whether your parent is sober and giving you sober advice or if you parent is making decisions while under the influence of a drug. Take good care of yourself.

In my school the popular kids all experiment with drugs. If I want to be popular how can I avoid experimenting with drugs?

It depends what your definition of popular is. These so called popular teenagers are at risk of getting arrested, damaging their health, their repuation, their school record and being in car accidents. Some may even die.

There are teenagers everywhere who do not want to do drugs or drink. Many churches and synagogues have great gathering places for teenagers. Community centers have dances. You may want to look at theater groups and teen orchestras. Frequently teenagers do community work in hospitals or are members in their school's peer group.

What are peer groups?

Peer groups are youth helping other youth work out conflict. Older students are usually trained by a counselor in school to help younger students resolve their concerns. Peer helpers often become preventive agents who recognize difficulties and encourage others to seek help from the appropriate professionals. Peer helpers offer emotional support and knowledge which translates to reduced drug and alcohol involvement, better study habits, unwanted pregnancies and reduced HIV/AIDS. Peer helpers increase their own self-esteem, morals and values. Peer workers generally become friends and learn how to make new friends among those who have their same outlook on life. It is not unusual that those who were befriended by a peer helper later on become themselves peer helpers.

Our school does not have a peer group. How can we start one?

Ask a favorite teacher or a counselor to start such a program. Look up The National Peer Helpers Association listed at the end of this book. NPHA will provide you and your teachers with all the necessary information.

What do teenagers who want to be in a peer group actually do?

There are various needs. The following story is a good example.

Marjory, a senior in high school, told how the school asked her to help Gloria, a freshman.

"My school counselor called me in, described the peer program to me, and asked if I would be willing to help Gloria who was somewhat shy. I attended three learning sessions with some other volunteers. We were told what to do in emergencies, about drugs and other dangers. I found the information especially interesting because my own mother is a recovered alcoholic who attends A.A. regularly. I have not been very good about going to Alateen.

I spent little time with Gloria but I did give her my home phone number. One day while I was home doing my homework Gloria phoned. She told me that her mother and her boyfriend were smoking pot. I told her to meet me at the school gym where I knew the varsity basketball team was practicing. As we sat and watched the team Gloria told me that her mother's boyfriend usually left at 7PM because he had a night job at the supermarket. I phoned my own family and told them I would be late. We watched the team and then we went out to a snack bar where we talked some more. I was shocked and felt sorry for Gloria. I told her about my own mother and how discouraged I was until my mother finally sought help and stopped drinking. I encouraged Gloria to confide more in our school counselor. When Gloria finally got home she phoned me to thank me and to tell me that her mother was home alone and asleep.

I did not feel sure about how I had handled the whole situation. I went to see our school counselor and told her the story. She smiled and said she could not have done better."

I am a sixteen-year-old girl who is happy to get out of the house whenever I can. Sometimes when I date, I stay out all night. My mother then calls me names. What right does my mother, as a substance abuser, have to think poorly of me?

There may be several reasons for your mother's behavior. She may feel guilty because of her own actions as a teenager. She may furthermore feel guilty about her own drugging and how her habit influenced her parenting.

In spite of all this heavy baggage your mother has, she may sincerely be worried about where you spend your nights. She may suspect you are engaged in sexual activity she feels is harmful to you.

Your mother may be ill, but she is still a parent. When your mother is sober, discuss with her what dating was like in her day and how she feels about dating today. Once you discuss dating with your mother, you may find her attitude changing more to your point of view. You might also find that some of her questions are valid and that you have been using her drugging as an excuse to avoid facing criticism.

What are some of the concerns my mother may have?

Primarily, a parent is concerned about risky people in your environment whose sexual behavior may endanger you. If you do not have a partner who is steady only with you, who uses condoms and who has been checked out by a doctor, there is a chance that you may get AIDS. You can also contract gonorrhea, herpes, which may later lead to cancer, syphilis, which can be fatal, or chlamydia, which can leave you infertile.

Your mother may also feel that you could get tied down with an unexpected pregnancy. She may be worried about how much your partner considers your feelings. All those endearing words he says are a responsibility. She may wonder about your own promises of love and if it may lead to an unwanted marriage.

Deep down your mother knows that because of her drugging your home has not been a stable home and that you may be looking for nothing more than to have someone take care of you.

A good rule of thumb is to finish your education and to be in counseling where you can discuss your hurts, and the poor values and habits you may have picked up at home. Your therapist may ask you to make a family diagram and to distinguish between inherited traits and acquired habits. She will point out how substance abuse in your family influenced your ability to communicate, build up defenses, feelings of low esteem, poor trust, and perhaps gender role confusion.

My father is an alcoholic. I am eighteen and want to get married. Both my parents say I am too young. In our state, you do not need permission to get married when you are eighteen, so I think I will just go ahead without my parents' blessings.

Deep down, your parents know their home has been a chaotic one. They may not know why their home has been a chaotic, but are concerned about what their home has done to you and whether you are ready for marriage.

Sometimes boys and girls are discouraged by the chaos at home. They hope that marriage will solve their problems. Marriage makes them feel someone cares and gives them the hope of having a trouble-free home of their own.

Too often, when we have not worked out the confusion and the unhappiness we saw at home, we not only bring our troubles into our marriage but also find it difficult to cope with the new responsibilities marriage has brought us.

If your parents do not approve of your upcoming marriage, and you do not see eye to eye with your parents, at least talk to a marriage counselor or to a clergyperson you have confidence in to get another objective viewpoint.

Marriage is a highly personal matter. Couldn't counseling only destroy the romance and love between two people?

Counseling will only strengthen and mature your love. A counselor will give you the confidence to know you are marrying for the right reasons.

Give a case history of how substance abuse in the home affected a teenager's decision to marry.

There are many, many case histories, and each one is different. The following is just one of these:

"I wish somebody had talked to me about dating when I was fifteen or had told me to read up on dating. My mother was an alcoholic, and my father had walked out on us. I could not stand to see my mother drink. When things were bad at home, I would run out with the first date available. Anything to get out. If any young person were to ask me today what to do when things are bad at home, I would say, 'Don't go out on a date for the sake of a date. Go to old friends to whom you can talk, join Alateen, or stay overnight with a family who knows your situation at home.'

"I didn't. One day I met a man fifteen years older than I. He was divorced and knew what life was about. I admired him. He was for me what I had always wanted — a father. He gave me the affection and admiration I didn't get at home. He gave me the advice I didn't get at home.

"My mother did not approve of him. She said he was too old for me. But there was a wonderful feeling in knowing someone was always ready to go out with me. When I think back, I didn't really love him. I just did not want to be bothered to look for other people to date. It was the first time in my life I had a shoulder to cry on, and I thought that was enough. We got married when I was seventeen and, now, at eighteen, I have a baby. There is not enough money because he has to pay alimony to his first wife and child. I have to work as a waitress at night to make ends meet. There does not seem to be time or money for going out even to a movie. On Sunday I am alone because he goes to visit his other child. Now that we are married, I don't enjoy his know-it-all attitude, which made me feel so secure before we were married. I wish I had someone close to my age who understands how I think.

"I feel that my friends are having fun dancing, traveling, studying, or working exciting jobs or buying pretty clothes while I am stuck at home. I feel that my future has been shortchanged."

My mother is a substance abuser. She smokes marijuana and takes pills. I got into trouble because my mother encouraged me to start dating at the age of twelve. What caused her to get me to date so young?

Your mother may have felt bad that you could not have friends to your house because of her drugging. Dating may have made your mother feel as if you belonged to a group and, in general, were accepted by society.

I am a sixteen-year-old girl. When my first date came to my house to pick me up, my father, who was drunk, fell down the front stairs. When we tried to help him up, he became abusive. What can girls in this situation do when their dates expect to pick them up at home?

When a boy takes you out for the first time and your alcoholic parent is drinking, offer to meet him elsewhere. If your alcoholic parent begins to drink a few hours before you expect your date, you can avoid the problem by phoning your date at his home to say your plans have changed, and ask him if he would mind meeting you elsewhere. It can be a girlfriend's house, a relative's house, or a reputable place in the center of town. Your date may ask you why he cannot come to your house. Should you feel at this point that you don't want to confide in him, you can make up a plausible excuse, such as, "I am at a girlfriend's house because she asked me to help her baby sit for her younger sister until you come." Those teenage girls who meet their date away from home should realize that their parents might feel worried about who their date is and where they are meeting him. Remember, even though a parent is an alcoholic, he feels responsible for you. It is understandable that you may not always like the manner in which your parent's illness causes him to show parental concern, but concern it is. It is wise to tell your parents, or at least your sober parent, who your date is, where you are going, and why they shouldn't worry. "We are not driving" or "He is an excellent driver" or "You know that I am very careful" are comments that may lessen their fears. You may want to leave them a written note where you can be reached and you may want to phone them during your date to put them at ease.

If your parents do have objections, however, you must think them over carefully. Let your parents feel that you want them to meet your date. You might say, "As soon as you stop drinking, I'll bring him home." Such comments may motivate your parent to stop drinking. Whatever you do, do not use the fact that you are meeting your dates on the outside as a weapon to criticize your parents. You can make your parents aware that the reason you don' t bring friends home is not because you are not proud of your parents, but because alcoholism is a disease that does not show them in their true light.

Both my parents are substance abusers. I am dating a girl I really like. I am afraid if I tell her my parents do drugs, she may lose interest in me. Should I keep dating her without telling her about my parents?

It is not necessary to tell a girl you take out the first or second time about your problems at home. But if you are going steady, exchanging intimate information is part of being close to each other.

Her real worry will be if you will copy your parents and also do drugs. However, if you explain to her that you do not want to touch drugs and alcohol–and show by your action by not even having a beer she will have confidence in your relationship.

One teenager told how he was very shy about telling his new girlfriend about his parents' drugging. When he finally started to tell her, she interrupted him. Instead, she poured her heart out about how her parents, who do not do drugs and only drink socially, either fight or do not talk at all to each other and were on the verge of divorce. Her problem had nothing to do with drugs but seemed just as hard to her. She was glad to have a boyfriend who could understand her. Being an understanding person and knowing how to explain your life at home will help you when dating.

10

Can Addiction be Cured?

CAN SUBSTANCE ABUSERS be cured?

As far as we know the only way a substance abuser can return to normal life is by giving up drugs and alcohol completely. Often drug abusers and alcoholics need to seek help.

I have heard that when substance abusers give up drugs or alcohol they experience withdrawal syndromes. What is meant by withdrawal syndromes?

Withdrawal syndromes are reactions that occur when a drug or alcohol is taken away from a person who is accustomed to its regular use.

It is as if the brain had a thermostat that was set higher because it was expecting to be slowed down by a drug. Once the brain has become adapted by regular use of drugs, a big rebound occurs when it is taken away. Without drugs, all the brain functions increase for a period of time until the thermostat readjusts.

How do these withdrawal syndromes appear?

In mild cases, withdrawal syndromes cause tremors, sweating or shaking of the hands. The withdrawal syndromes can also result in the person seeing things that aren't there (hallucinations), in convulsions that are just like epileptic seizures, and, in the most serious cases, in delirium tremens (DTs).

My father is an alcoholic. He is afraid to stop drinking because of DTs. What happens when an alcoholic has DTs?

This is the most serious type of withdrawal reaction. It usually starts about one to three days after drinking has ceased. The patient should be in a hospital. If a doctor can't be found, the police will help to get him to the hospital.

The withdrawal may start with a convulsion. The alcoholic begins hearing, feeling, and seeing things that aren't there. The alcoholic is disoriented and doesn't know where he is or what is happening. He may be very frightened. He has a rapid pulse count, profuse sweating, and a high fever. Doctors know how to ease these symptoms. However, fearing DTs is only an excuse for not stopping to drink.

Other drugs such as sedatives and sleeping pills may also produce difficult withdrawals.

Heroin addicts suffer bone pain, muscle spasms, abdominal cramps, diarrhea, and sweating.

Serious substance abusers can place themselves in a clinic where these symptoms can be monitored and treated before they get out of hand.

What are convulsions?

A convulsion is a "mass discharge" of signals from the overactive brain. The person loses consciousness, the body undergoes a rhythmical series of muscular contractions, the eyes may turn to one side. Then the body stiffens to a very rigid position with all the muscles contracted, and breathing stops. After this, there is a relaxation of the muscles and deep breathing. Within a short time the person may awaken and will not remember what happened. The convulsion may repeat, or there may only be one.

What can one do to help the drug addict when he or she has a convulsion?

Phone 911.

What are some steps that can be taken to help an alcoholic or drugging parent?

The first and most important step is for the whole family to recognize that the parent is ill and has lost control.

The second step is for the drug abuser to want to do something about the disease. The substance abuser is the only one who can conquer his addiction. There are hospitals, clinics, social and religious agencies, and groups such as Alcoholics Anonymous, Marijuana Anonymous, and Narcotics Anonymous to help those suffering from addiction. The substance abuser will usually seek out these agencies once he has realized this is an illness. The family members have to realize that their encouragement while the substance abuser is seeking help can aid the person in conquering his dependency on drugs or alcohol.

The earlier a family recognizes a substance abuser in their midst, the easier it will be for them to cope with the disease and perhaps make the addict aware that there is hope.

My father is an addicted gambler. He became furious when I told him to seek help. Why can't I get through to him?

Your father misunderstood what you were trying to tell him. Your father, at this point, is still afraid of the future. He worries about how he could live without his gambling. He still does not have enough insight into his illness to ask himself why he gambles and to face the fact that he is ruining his family.

This is an illness like alcoholism or drug addiction and you are asking too much of yourself to tackle this powerful disease. Try and talk to a school counselor, to Gamblers Anonymous or to Gam-Anon, a group geared to helping the families of gamblers. They may know how to make your father aware of his serious condition. All these organizations are listed in Chapter 14.

If the family does not succeed in making the substance abuser realize he or she is ill, should a son or daughter seek someone outside the family to talk to the addict?

It might help, provided the person you seek out has knowledge of addiction. If you get someone who warns the addicted with "Pull yourself together" or "Aren't you ashamed of yourself?" more damage than good can be done.

Do not be upset if the first person you go to for help does not understand your problem at home. They may be good friends and wonderful people, but they may not have had experience in confronting addiction. Do not give up. Go talk to your family doctor, or a counselor at school. Perhaps your clergyperson has had experience with addicts. You also might try an intervention.

What is an intervention?

An intervention is a process involving a trained (very important) interventionist, family, and/ or close friends who come together in a hopefully loving, caring way to confront the drug abuser and to introduce change in his life and consequently to the family he lives with.

Before such a confrontation can take place the family and his friends have to do a lot of work with a trained interventionist. The family has to decide together with the trained interventionist what is the best time to do this and where the drug abuser will go immediately after the intervention—a hospital or a rehabilitation center or a daily outpatient clinic. The interventionist will probably ask the family to write a history of the substance abuser and how his drug taking affected his children, the rest of the family, their friends, his colleagues, and his work.

When the intervention finally takes place with a counselor there, it will be a safe place for you to tell your drinking and/or drug taking parent how you have been hurt, how you have been denied a parent, how you have not had the youth you deserve, how the drug taking has interfered with your social life, your ability to study, and how you are no longer going to deny the problem.

One of the greatest accomplishments of intervention is that it stops denial. Denial is the most destructive aspects of addiction. It denies healing and it involves lying.

I have told my father over and over what I think of his drug taking. Why do we need a trained interventionist?

Because reason and discussion often don't work and lead to frustration and anger. A family has to live with the abuser's arguments. The abuser may be so used to the family's urgings that he may not pay attention to them anymore. It is one of the "family dances" that a good intervention should stop. An interventionist knows how to organize several people meaningful to the substance abuser to talk in an effective, controlled, and logical way that will break through the denial pattern. A group of ten people is more influential than just four or five members trying to convince the addict that he needs help. If members of Alcoholics Anonymous or Narcotics Anonymous are in the group they will know how to talk the addict's language.

When a friend speaks, the drug abuser cannot help but take note that his indulgence has gone so far that even friends are concerned about him.

If a physician is included she can give a medical diagnosis that the person is a drug abuser and let him know that if he is willing to cooperate, a proper course of action can be prescribed.

A clergyperson he trusts can draw on the experience of dealing with other drug abusers in the parish. He might introduce him to other recovering drug abusers who would help him realize that there are others afflicted with this disease, and who are succeeding in recovering their health.

The cohesion and purposefulness of the group breaks through that feeling of helplessness and anger. The interventionist needs to be there because she is trained to talk to a drug-dependent parent who may act abusively when in need of drugs.

We had an intervention. Everything went as planned. My mother agreed to go to a treatment center. We went to Nar Anon and several times a week to a program in the drug clinic where my mother was a patient to learn how to deal with the disease and what it had done to us. We ran the household carefully with my father. My mother came home and after about three months we found that she was smoking marijuana again. So what good was the intervention?

Relapses are common among drug-dependent patients and should not be considered a negative. Your parent may believe that she has the power to use the substance safely after a period of sobriety. A relapse reminds her that she will always have the disease and cannot use the substance.

The intervention did plant a seed in your mother's mind. It gave you the opportunity to tell her how you felt about her smoking and you yourself learned that you can have a healthy life and do not have to repeat your mother's habits. But most of all your mother needs more treatment and you should discuss this with your counselor and your father. Did your mother go regularly to Narcotics Anonymous after she came home?

What is Narcotics Anonymous?

NA is a nonprofit fellowship or society of men and women for whom drugs had become a major problem. Membership is open to any drug addict regardless of the particular drug or combination of drugs used. NA members live by the same Twelve-Step program that Alcoholics Anonymous uses.

What exactly does Alcoholics Anonymous do?

Alcoholics Anonymous is a worldwide fellowship of men and women who help each other to maintain sobriety and who offer to share their recovery experience freely with others who may have a substance abuse or drinking problem. The group was started to help alcoholics. At each meeting alcoholics tell how they managed to stop their habit and how long they have been sober. It can be a day or years.

When an alcoholic comes to A.A. and says he or she would like to try to stop drinking, the addict is introduced to a sponsor. The sponsor is a person experienced in the Twelve Steps and helps the new member by teaching the tools of A.A. The alcoholic may phone the sponsor, who is a fellow recovered alcoholic, whenever — no matter what time of day or night — the urge to take a drink cannot be controlled.

Some are afraid to join Alcoholics Anonymous because they fear they will "slip" (relapse) and start their habit again and that their group might lose confidence in them. People in A.A. never judge or give up. Alcoholics in A.A. whose drinking has been arrested understand the slips, the good and the bad moods, because they have experienced them, too.

The program includes "Twelve Suggested steps" to help the alcoholic maintain sobriety. The most important step is the first one: "We admitted we were powerless over alcohol, that our lives had become unmanageable." With this step the physical illness is arrested if the person stops drinking. The other eleven steps help the newcomer to deal with his emotional and spiritual illness.

Alcoholics Anonymous has excellent literature that explains in great detail how the program helps the alcoholic. Once you receive this literature, the other members in your immediate family might also be interested in reading it. After seeing it, the one who needs A.A. might even be encouraged to seek help.

A.A. literature is available at your local A.A. meetings. If you do not find A.A. listed in your local phone book, its main phone number and Internet sites are listed at the end of this book.

Narcotics Anonymous and Marijuana Anonymous have based their organizations on the A.A. method.

Do teenagers ever visit A.A., Narcotics Anonymous or Marijuana Anonymous?

Yes. You will feel welcomed at all these organizations and might meet other teenagers who are in the same predicament as you. It is not unusual for teenagers to go to open meetings to listen and to talk to recovering substance abusers. Such a visit will give you hope that your parents, too, can regain their health, and by listening to the substance abusers present, you will gain insight into their suffering.

What do they do at the closed meetings?

The same as at the open meetings, but new members sometimes feel freer to work out their problems when they are among fellow substance abusers only.

Do women also attend Alcoholics Anonymous, Marijuana Anonymous, and Narcotics Anonymous?

Yes. All these organizations are for both men and women. Women usually have a female sponsor; men, a male. There are as well all female meetings, all male meetings and mixed meetings. Some towns have as many as fifteen meetings going on throughout the day.

What type of person is a sponsor in A.A.?

A sponsor is a fellow citizen in your town who has an alcohol problem similar to that of your parent. The sponsor is a fellow member in A.A. who has "worked" the Twelve Steps and who has at least a year of sobriety. You will find that A.A. has many active, honored, and talented citizens in your town. What impresses and encourages the new A.A. members is how the sponsors, who once had the same problem as the new members, now look healthy, are full of pep and zest, and appear happy.

I am afraid to visit any self-help group because it may get around town that we have a problem at home. What should I do?

If someone should see you walk into an A.A. meeting or any abuse help group, that person will not know who you are going for. You might go because you are writing a paper for school or because you are concerned about a friend. There is a saying at these self-help groups: "Who you see here, and what you hear here, when you leave here, let it stay here."

Are A.A., N.A., or M.A. the only sources of help available to the alcoholic and/or substance abuser?

There are many other sources of help. Many hospitals and clinics have facilities and medical aid available to the substance abuser. Most states today have extensive substance-abuse and/or alcoholism programs set up in conjunction with their state university or with their public health, mental health, or social welfare departments.

Many medical complexes have A.A.,N.A., and M.A. meetings for their patients. These patients hopefully will continue to go to these meetings once they leave the hospital.

Do Alcoholics Anonymous, Narcotics Anonymous, or Marijuana Anonymous have any religious affiliation?

Many people mistakenly think that these organizations are run by a religious group. They are not allied with any sect, denomination, political organization, or institution.

Are Alcoholics Anonymous, Narcotics Anonymous, or Marijuana Anonymous expensive?

There are no fees or dues. A basket is passed at each meeting, but nobody looks to see if everyone gives or how much one gives.

Why do Alcoholics Anonymous, Heroin Anonymous, Gamblers Anonymous or Marijuana Anonymous meet separately?

Alcoholics Anonymous was founded in 1935. The backbone of A.A. are the Twelve Steps. Other substance abusers soon realized that the Twelve Steps could help them too and started to form their own meetings. Those with cross addiction choose sometimes to go only to A.A and make the A.A. program work for all their addictions. It is important to remember that Narcotics Anonymous helps all substance abusers, is well represented throughout the United States, and has a program, Nar Anon, to help the families of substance abusers.

How are substance abusers and alcoholics treated at a clinic or hospital?

The clinic takes the history of the patient: when and how he started his substance abuse, how long he has been drugging and/or drinking heavily, the pattern, and his life history in general. The clinic finds out what past stresses he experienced in school, in his career, with parents and his present family, and with the opposite sex.

The clinic may choose to interview a relative to get a wider perspective and may encourage and offer therapy to the whole family so that they can work out their own hurt that comes from living with a substance abuser.

Those who interviewed the patient will assess his case at a staff meeting so that the best course of action may be decided on. After detoxification, the hospital or clinic may recommend twenty-eight-day in-patient rehabilitation. Included will be group therapy and perhaps individual therapy.

An outpatient follow-up program is nearly always recommended. Clinics do have, in most instances, their own outpatient programs.

Is there a central agency where I can find out about all the facilities in our town for substance abusers or alcoholics?

Phone a medical facility. Look in your local phone book under the words Drug, Alcohol, Addiction, or Alcoholism Information Center. Check the resource list at the end of this book.

11

When a Parent Stops Drugging and/or Drinking

WHAT MOTIVATES A substance abuser finally to stop?

The substance abuser's own realization that she cannot use drugs and/or alcohol safely and that her addiction can be helped if she has the honest desire to stop drugging and/or drinking.

My father used to take drugs. He is so ill-tempered that I think life was easier while he was taking drugs. What is making him so moody and difficult?

The convalescing period is frequently a very long and difficult time for the substance abuser. Your father is still experiencing tensions and depressions. Among other things he is trying to deal with his emotions without using drugs. Attending Narcotics Anonymous meetings will help your father greatly with these problems.

You need to take care of your own well being and should be attending Nar Anon or other groups mentioned in Chapter 14 that help the families of addicts to deal with their own pain.

What, in general, is involved in a substance abuser's recovery period?

A substance abuser and/or alcoholic's recovery consists generally of four phases. The first, as we have already mentioned, is the substance abuser's acceptance that he can no longer control his substance abuse. He admits to himself that he has a problem with drugs and/ or alcohol and surrenders to it. During this first stage, the abuser may gain hope by meeting recovering alcoholics and drug abusers who are normal and happy. Help can also come through an understanding clergyperson, counselor, or psychiatrist.

During this period it is recommended that he go to a medical doctor to get a thorough checkup. He may need vitamins after many years of poor eating, or some of the internal organs may have been affected by the drug use and heavy drinking and may need treatment.

In the second phase, the substance abuser begins to share his life with the family and breaks through the isolation that he has experienced. He begins to see that he drugged and/or drank to cope with feelings of hopelessness and sense of failure, for example.

As time goes on, the substance abuser will enter the third phase, which starts when he gets to know himself better. He begins to have a new awareness of "pressure points," the kind of thinking and emotional reactions that have pressured him to use drugs and alcohol. As the therapy continues, he will grow emotionally, take stress better, and desire the escape of substance abuse less and less. The third step is really the core of the recovery process.

In the final stage, the substance abuser gains confidence in his ability to work; he wants to help others with their problem of substance abuse and is willing to continue getting therapy or counseling when the desire to do drugs or drink arises.

How long does the convalescing period take?

Each substance abuser needs a different amount of time. The whole convalescing period can take anywhere from three months to two years.

How does one know when the substance abuser is rehabilitated?

Substance abusers say that when they feel sobriety is preferable to their old life they are on the way to a safe recovery.

My mother is an alcoholic. She did not touch a drink for two years, and we all felt she had complete insight into her alcoholism. One day, for no reason in particular, she went back to drinking. How can such behavior be explained?

As with any disease, relapses may occur. Giving up her therapy too soon or not attending A.A. meetings can be a mistake. Gradually, as your mother continues with her therapy, she will realize that drinking will not solve her problems, and her bouts should become fewer. This is true for all substance abusers.

Is there any way a family can recognize a substance abuser's anxieties?

Yes. Signs of anxieties are pacing, clenching of a fist, or extreme silences or talkativeness. If the substance abuser smokes, you'll note an increase in his use of his cigarettes, cigars, or pipes.

What can a family do to alleviate a substance abuser's anxieties?

Substance abusers need to live through their anxities to get better. However, you should show faith in the ability of the drugging or drinking parent whenever possible. Comments like "Mom, I am so glad you haven't had a drink or taken pills in six months" will make it all worthwhile to her. If an alcoholic father makes a good barbecue, or you appreciate that he took you to the ball game, let him know it. As long as the comments are sincere, they will be effective. Substance abusers are sensitive people and can see through a compliment for the sake of a compliment.

My father is an alcoholic who has not touched a drink in fifteen months. The fact that he does not drink does not make him any fairer to his children. For instance, one day he says we may use the family car, and the next day, for no reason whatsoever, he will not let us use his car. What makes some alcoholic parents so inconsistent even after they have stopped drinking?

A parent may continue or retain the pattern of inconsistency he had while actively drinking or drugging, even when he is sober. Remember, alcoholism and drug abuse in some people are symptoms of not feeling comfortable with oneself or maybe even symptoms of mental illness. The patient may have drunk or taken drugs "to feel better." In such a situation, it is wise to take each permission to do something as an individual occasion, as the rule of the day, or even, the moment. Those who attend Alcoholics Anonymous or, as the need may be, Narcotics Anonymous and "work the program," namely the Twelve Steps, do begin to change.

Make your own life fuller by looking at the list of self-help organizations at the end of this book and find a group of teenagers who have the same problems as you and who want to talk.

12

Counseling for the Teenager

WHAT DOES COUNSELING for the teenager involve?

The counselor listens. The counselor is interested in what worries you, what the complaints are, what you have lived through. The counselor helps a person to vent feelings and think through the best course of action.

A counselor may help you to understand you are not the reason for the drugging or excessive drinking in your home and help you to understand your own reaction to it. While the counselor will not tell you what to do, she may help you to understand the situation you live with and offer guidelines and some course of action for coping with such a dilemma.

Where can a teenager obtain counseling?

There are many services geared specifically to teenagers. First to be considered is Alateen, which consists of groups of teenagers who meet to discuss the problem of living with alcoholic parents. Sometimes teens whose parent may use other substances join this group. You might also consider getting in touch with National Council on Alcoholism and Drug Dependence, Inc., Nar Anon, and Hazelden all listed at the end of this book. Don't worry about cost. These organizations do not charge.

Most substance-abuse clinics in your community will have family programs. Feel free to call a clinic even if your parent is not yet in recovery.

Furthermore, many churches, community centers, teenage recreation centers, and family service agencies sponsor teenage walk-in services. These walk-in services are prepared to deal with all kinds of problems, not just substance abuse.

Why is it called "teenage walk-in center"?

Because a teenager can walk in without an appointment and talk to a counselor about anything that he or she may be concerned with.

Who are the counselors?

The counselors are professionals who are certified in counseling.

Are there other kids around when I talk to the counselor?

The counselor talks to you alone in a private room. In addition, some walk-in centers offer group rap sessions for those teenagers who enjoy it.

If I go to a walk-in center, will my parents be involved?

These centers do not phone your parents unless you want them to be involved. Sometimes these counselors can reach a parent when a son or daughter cannot. Experience has taught the counselors that even the most difficult, ill-tempered parents are not beyond help, but can be helped by a therapist who knows how to relate them.

My parents are so impossible that no counselor can talk to them. What does the center do when parents are beyond help?

Not all family problems are solved easily. A teenager may come from a home where he simply cannot thrive because the environment does not meet his needs. The center will discuss with such families the advantages of boarding schools or the possibility that the teenager might live with a favorite relative.

If a case is very difficult, and the parents do not cooperate, the center may place a teenager with a "host," or foster family, until the parents are able to resume their responsibilities. The center may discuss with the teenager whether he wants to leave home and refer him to the proper social agency that has the legal power to move him out of his home. Many times, the counselor works overtime to help.

What is a host family?

A host family is a family living in or near your community that is willing and able to offer their home on very short notice to a teenager who may need a place to stay for a night or two.

Both my parents are substance abusers. I hate it at home. I don't want to wait until some agency decides where I should go. As long as I can hitchhike, I can make my way.

Before you do anything, speak to a counselor you trust, find out what the laws are concerning minors in your state, and consider the alternatives to running away. A counselor will tell you how life can be made more tolerable at home or at least help you leave with an open door behind you in case you want to come back.

Many teenagers say that running away is the quickest and easiest solution to unpleasant family problems. The open road may look attractive, but many that have walked it have told stories of lives spent in fear. If they are underage and someone robs them or abuses them, they are afraid to call the police for fear they will be caught. This makes them easy prey for thieves and other criminals.

If you do get caught, you take a chance of being put in a detention center or a state institution, some of which are excellent. However, if you are the one to approach a counselor, you can discuss with her what facilities are available without having a court decide where you should go.

I feel like a weirdo having to go to a counselor for help. Why should I even consider it?

It is understandable to find it difficult to seek out a counselor. It may be easier to speak to an adult you do trust—a teacher, a relative, some one at Alateen or Nar Anon — and ask him or her to help you find a counselor. The advantage to going to a substance-abuse counselor is that she will know the best ways to handle your situation.

Where can I find out whether there is a walk-in center in our town or any other counseling facility geared to teenagers?

Very often walk-in centers place posters in the schools. Phone your local "hot line." Look up family service, or youth service, in your local phone book. Check out the Internet. Study the resources listed at the end of this book. Ask your local newspaper, library, school counselor, clergyperson, physician, mental health association, or teacher what services exist for those who want help. Just don't give up if the first place you go to isn't for you.

What is a hot line?

A hot line is a telephone number a teenager can dial. The person who answers is a fellow teenager or a counselor who knows about the various facilities in the town. The person who answers the phone will give any immediate advice or comfort needed. Names of the callers are never asked.

What is family therapy?

Family therapy is a form of psychotherapy. All it means is that the family all gets together to discuss their thoughts, problems, and ideas with an objective counselor. The goal behind this is for family members to learn to relate and function better as a family.

Each family has its own way of doing things and reacting to life's problems. When an objective person is present, the family can learn to see its own strengths and weaknesses and learn as one unit how to help themselves. Parents often come out of these sessions with a better understanding of how drugging has hurt their children. And the children gain insight into their parents' problems and what they, as children, can do to lessen the tension and strife at home.

Both my parents are substance abusers. I contacted family service and I am seeing a counselor there. My older sister thinks it is disgusting that I tell my counselor about our family. My sister needs help as much as I do. How can I get her to come to a family service agency?

Your sister's feelings describe many teenagers' feelings. She may think her problems are unique, or that it is a sign of weakness to seek help. She may feel the group will judge her. Instead of showing compassion, she fears the agency or the professional giving guidance might only point out the faults and mistakes of the family members.

Your sister will have the courage to seek help once she sees it as a way to get more information about how to handle her life. Her story will be respected and will not invade the family privacy. No professional person can reveal confidential information for both ethical and legal reasons. For instance, no report may be automatically released to your parents without you signing a release unless—and this is important—you are planning to hurt yourself and/or others. A counselor is also under legal obligation to report child abuse (including sexual abuse), and child neglect. But this is all very positive because you will get the help and care you need.

The more you share your experience of seeking help with your sister, the less guarded she will be.

My father is an alcoholic. My mother says she knows all about counseling, but she won't let me go. How can I convince my mother to let me go to counseling or to Alateen?

On occasion, one will hear of cases where a teenager realizes his or her parent is sick and would like to seek help, but one or both parents are against seeking help. In these cases, the parents have not yet accepted alcoholism or substance abuse as a disease. They may feel ashamed of the problem at home. They may think that by keeping the problem quiet and acting as if nothing is wrong, they will not lose face in the community. Moreover, your mother may feel the reason you want to seek help is because she has failed you as a mother — not because of alcoholism. In these cases it is wise to send for brochures on alcoholism from the nearest Alcoholics Anonymous office, Al-Anon, or from your nearest branch of National Council on Alcoholism and Drug Dependence Inc., and show them to your parents. Perhaps you can convince your mother to go to the open monthly meetings of Alateen, where guests are welcomed. Very often a teenager will find that one or both parents are so bogged down by their problems that they do not have the time, or a clear head, to think objectively about any organization.

If you do decide to go to counseling or to join Alateen, be careful that you do not let your parents feel you are seeking help for them. You are going for help because the pressures that come with the disease have hurt you, too. Remember too that you can always get more information on the Internet.

13

Alateen and Other Programs

HOW DID ALATEEN start?

Alateen is an outgrowth of Al-Anon. Al-Anon was organized by wives and husbands of those alcoholics attending Alcoholics Anonymous. The purpose of both Al-Anon and Alateen is to help those living with an alcoholic regain their inner strength and stability.

Before Alateen existed, a parent was always encouraged to bring his teenager along to Al-Anon, but teenagers found it hard to discuss their problems at Al-Anon meetings when one of their own parents was listening. In 1957 a young California boy, who felt that the problem of the teenager with an alcoholic father or mother was different from the nonalcoholic wife or husband, founded a new group that came to be known as Alateen.

What actually happens when you join Alateen?

Alateen can change your life. In Alateen you can talk to other teenagers who also have an alcoholic parent. Alateens encourage one another and learn effective ways to cope with their problems.

Alateens air their problems of living with an alcoholic. Each member realizes that other teenagers also have moments when it is difficult for them to act properly toward their ill parent. In talking to these teenagers, you will find that your personal experience can help them, too.

In all discussions, last names are never mentioned and specific personal acts are never described. The sponsor of each Alateen group, who is an Alcoholics Anonymous member, Al-Anon member, or an understanding experienced Alateen member, helps to lead the discussions. Alateens will sometimes have parents come from Alcoholics Anonymous to describe what they went through before they stopped drugging or drinking. This is always a marvelous opportunity to ask questions.

Teenagers who belong to Alateen never feel alone. They make new friends. When they visit each other, no one has to explain why a parent in the home is ill. In between group meetings, when things are rough at home, these teenagers can phone the group's sponsor or a fellow member to discuss the immediate problem without interfering in the parent's way of life. For example, if a member has a geometry exam to cram for, and a parent is out of control, an experienced Alateen member will not tell the parent to stop, but will focus her concern on the fellow member. If he is upset, a fellow

Alateen member might calm him by reminding him that the parent is ill and that the parent has to come to his own decision to do something about his substance abuse. If necessary, she will get the teenager out of the house and help to find a peaceful place to study, be it the library or another member's home. Should a teenager find the situation at home intolerable because a parent is abusive, a fellow Alateen member may offer her home until the parent sobers up.

Is that the whole Alateen program?

No. Besides having a sponsor and meetings, they follow the same twelve steps as Alcoholics Anonymous and believe in living "one day at a time."

What is "one day at a time"?

"One day at a time" means that Alateens deal with each day as it comes. You can endure something for twenty-four hours. There is always hope that the next day might be completely different. Alateens feel, why waste your precious energy worrying about the unknown when you can put that energy to use to make today better?

Do Alateens pray?

Like Alcoholics anonymous, Alateens say they are a nonreligious group. Each member interprets the concept of a higher power differently.

My parent uses marijuana. Can I go to Alateen?

Alateen was founded for and by families of alcoholics. No one is ever turned away. However there are other programs geared to help families of substance abusers using the same Twelve Step method, the serenity prayer, and living "one day at a time" as Alateen. Nar Anon is one such program. If you can't find anything near you, get in touch with National Council on Alcoholism and Drug Dependencies. Their 800 number is listed in the next chapter and they'll know of an appropriate group in your area.

It seems all these programs use the Twelve Steps. What actually are the Twelve Steps?

As stated previously many other organizations use the Twelve Steps substituting the word alcohol with "marijuana," "heroin," "crack" and so on. I do believe some organizations have altered other words and added more words to fit their needs. The following are the original Twelve Steps published by Alcoholics Anonymous.

1. We admitted we were powerless over alcohol — that our lives had become unmanageable.

2. Came to believe that a Power greater than ourselves could restore us to sanity.

3. Made a decision to turn our will and our lives over to the care of God as we understood Him.

4. Made a searching and fearless moral inventory of ourselves.

5. Admitted to God, to ourselves and to another human being the exact nature of our wrongs.

6. Were entirely ready to have God remove all these defects of character.

7. Humbly asked Him to remove our shortcomings.

8. Made a list of all persons we had harmed, and became willing to make amends to them all.

9. Made direct amends to such people wherever possible, except when to do so would injure them or others.

10. Continued to take personal inventory and when we were wrong promptly admitted it.

11. Sought through prayer and meditation to improve our conscious contact with God as we understood Him, praying only for knowledge of His will for us and the power to carry that out.

12. Having had a spiritual awakening as the result of these steps, we tried to carry this message to alcoholics and to practice these principles in all our affairs.

I don't take drugs, my parents do. Why should I say I am powerless over alcohol, marijuana and so on?

Your parents' drugging has certainly effected your life, and in that sense, once you let go, admit your were powerless, you will experience a tremendous sense of relief. Each step can help those who live with the sick person. Each step will enrich your life, help you to be calm, enable you to express love and to reach your goals.

These Twelve Steps ask for a lot. Don't newcomers get discouraged?

Alcoholics Anonymous understand these feelings and this is how they explain it. Other organizations using The Twelve Steps give similar explanations.

The relative success of the A.A. program seems to be due to the fact that an alcoholic who no longer drinks has an exceptional faculty for "reaching" and helping an uncontrolled drinker.

In simplest form, the A.A. program operates when a recovered alcoholic passes along the story of his or her own problem drinking, describes the sobriety he or she has found in A.A., and invites the newcomer to join the informal Fellowship.

The heart of the suggested program of personal recovery is contained in Twelve Steps describing the experience of the earliest members of the Society:

Newcomers are not asked to accept or follow these Twelve Steps in their entirety if they feel unwilling or unable to do so.

They will usually be asked to keep an open mind, to attend meetings at which recovered alcoholics describe their personal experiences in achieving sobriety, and to read A.A. literature describing and interpreting the A.A. program.

A.A. members will usually emphasize to newcomers that only problem drinkers themselves, individually, can determine whether or not they are in fact alcoholics.

At the same time, it will be pointed out that all available medical testimony indicates that alcoholism is a progressive illness, that it cannot be cured in the ordinary sense of the term, but that it can be arrested through total abstinence from alcohol in any form.

I am exceptionally shy. I don't think that I could ever open my mouth at an Alateen or Nar Anon meeting. When one goes to an Alateen meeting is one asked to say anything?

No one is asked to talk. But you cannot help but participate, because as others talk your reaction will be: "The very same thing happened to me," or "Wait, let me tell you how I handled that same situation." You will develop an inner strength and confidence that you have never known before. Alateens plan fun, too. They have parties and barbecues that every member enjoys.

Where are Nar Anon, Alateen, and Al-Anon located?

They should be listed in your phone book under Nar Anon or Al-Anon, depending whether your parent is an alcoholic or substance abuser. Once you phone Al-Anon or Nar Anon, they will tell you where the nearest Alateen or Nar Anon is located. You can also touch base with them on the Internet. There are various chat groups on the web. If these organizations are not near, you can start one.

What do the mothers and fathers discuss in the closed meetings of Al-Anon or Nar Anon?

They discuss in part how to have better relationships with their children, how to have greater compassion for their son's and daughter's experiences with a parent's substance abuse, and how to help the substance abuser realize that she is ill, or, if she has stopped drinking or drugging, how to give support.

Does the fact that the sober parent goes to Al-Anon and the children to Alateen or, if need be, to Nar Anon have any effect on the alcoholic and/or substance abusing parent?

Quite often it does. When the substance abuser sees the family pull itself together and treat him with the knowledge that the compulsive drugging and/or drinking is a sickness, he may be motivated to seek help.

I get discouraged very easily. My father admits he is a substance abuser, but he has not stopped drugging. All these Alateen and Nar Anon lifestyles sound great, but how can I believe them when I see what goes on at home?

Go to Alateen if your parent is suffering from alcoholism and Nar Anon if your parent is taking marijuana, crack, heroin, or other drugs and you will find out it is possible to change your life. At each meeting you get new courage, more insight on how to handle your problems, how to cope with your sick parent, and above all, how to manage your personal life. At one Alateen meeting a girl pointed out, very sadly, that her father had gotten drunk again just when she thought he was going to make an effort to seek help. She also told the group that when he was recovering from the drinking bout, he talked to her as he had never talked to her before. He mentioned that he now considered his drinking an illness. Another girl at that Alateen meeting, whose father had not used heroin in two years, explained to her that things were not as glum as she thought. The fact that her father admitted that he was ill was a real step forward on his part, and she assured her that her father would eventually seek help. She pointed out that she should give her father more courage and more hope. The same is true for all addictions.

To believe Alateen and other help groups such as Nar Anon work, you have to go and experience it.

Suppose my father never stops drugging or drinking?

As you are growing up, you will make more and more friends outside of your family, you will date more, and in all likelihood, you will form a family of your own. You will have your career, your place to live, and you will be able to separate yourself from the problems at home. When you think of it, most children spend only eighteen or twenty years at home. They are important years because they are your formative years. But now that you are aware of what makes you tick and of people who want to help you, you can take the fruit of your experiences, the tough things you saw, as well as the positive and constructive experiences, and build them into the kind of life you always wanted for yourself. To help you along in adult life, you may want to join Al-Anon, Adult Children of Alcoholics or Nar Anon, or other support groups.

14

Internet and Helpful 800 Numbers

NOW THAT YOU know that you are not helpless, that there are other people who are willing to help, you may want to get in touch with some of the agencies listed here and share their addresses with others who are in a similar situation. Many teenagers belong to more than one support group because they get different vibrations, comfort, and information from each group.

Some of these resources have simple toll-free telephone numbers and parallel sites on the Internet. The 800 numbers are there for you if you prefer to talk on the phone. Your local telephone book has its own listings for Alateen, Al-Anon and Alcoholics Anonymous, Narcotics Anonymous, Drug Addiction and Gamblers Anonymous.

If you prefer to talk to someone out-of-town the main numbers and web sites are all listed here. I have put an asterisk next to those which are especially helpful if you are upset and need immediate information or have decided to seek help on a long term basis.

Each address and phone number comes with space for you to write your own personal notes. For instance you may find it helpful to write down the name of the person you spoke to and may want to speak to again. You may also want to jot down some advice, a helpful phone number, the name of a clinic, a counselor, and where the various groups meet in your area.

http://www.aa.org Alcoholics Anonymous; support groups for recovering alcoholics

http://www.aaip.com Association of American Indian Physicians; be sure to click on student activities.

http://www.aca-usa.org American Council on Alcoholism

*http://www.acde.org American Council for Drug Education; a confidential treatment referral service available 24 hours a day; has an online discussion group

http://www.addictionresourceguide.com A comprehensive directory of addiction treatment facilities listed online; a good start for finding intervention help

*http://www.al-anon.org Support group for family (including teenagers) of alcoholics

http://www.alcoholism.net

http://www.asam.org American Society of Addiction Medicine; an organization of doctors trained in addiction; an excellent place to look for medical information, counseling and intervention help; you can e-mail your questions

*http://www.bgca.org Boys and Girls Club of America; unique programs including family support, life skills and health

http://www.bolt.com A site for teenagers to hang out, speak out and find out

http:///www.caron.org A nonprofit addiction and chemically dependency treatment center providing services for adults and adolescents

http://www.cheekfreak.com/ Geared to teenagers — get help with problems, chat and post your art

*http://www.childhelpusa.org Help for adolescents and children who are being abused

*http://www.child.net For all ages — teenagers, adults and children — everything you can think of including music, games, fun and comprehensive information about drugs and living with a parent taking drugs

*http://www.coaf.org Among other services, help for teens on how to break the intergenerational cycle of substance abuse

http://www.co-anon.org A support group for the family of the substance abuser.

http://www.copes.org Information center for substance abuse

http://www.csat.org Center for substance abuse treatment; you can e-mail them for answers

**http://www.drughelp.org* Information about crisis intervention services *_http://www.factsontap.org_ Geared solely for children of alcoholics and other substance abusers

http://www.freedominstitute.org/ Freedom from alcohol and drug dependency with a special discussion forum for teens

*_http://www.Gam-Anon.org_ Help for the families of gamblers; you can e-mail any questions you have

http://www.gamblersanonymous.org Gamblers helping each other to overcome their habit *http://www.goosehead.com* A teen portal for excellent advice, chat, music and free mail

*http://www.hazelden.com A nonprofit organization dedicated to helping people recover from alcoholism and drug addiction; offers programs for families who have lived with a substance abuser; has on-line chat programs.

http://www.health.org National Clearinghouse for Alcohol and Drug Information

*http://www.health.org/nacoa/ National Association for Children of Alcoholics (and other drugs)

http://www.intervention.com Answers questions about what intervention is, when to use it, how to use it and where to get help

http://www.lowefamily.org Provided by the Lowe Family Foundation for families coping with alcoholism.

http://www.marijuana-anonymous.org Support groups for recovering marijuana addicts

http://www.mediacampaign.org National Youth Anti-Drug Media Campaign offers helpful insight into drug problems

nanacoa@nanacoa.org e-mail for National Association of Native American Children of Alcoholics

http://www.na.org Web site for Narcotics Anonymous, a community-based association of recovering addicts

http://www.naranon.com Support groups for family and friends of drug abusers

http://www.ncadd.org National Council on Alcoholism and Drug Dependencies—information and referrals for both the substance abuser and those who live with him or her

http://www.peerhelping.org Tells you everything you want to know about peer groups

**http://www.ola-is.org* Al-Anon on line with a special teen forum; for friends and family of the alcoholic

http://www.recoverycentral.org Good place to get answers about recovery

http://www.sada.org Students Against Drugs and Alcohol

*http://www.teen-anon.com A teenage friendly organization for those worried about their own or another friend's or family member's use of alcohol; based on the Twelve Steps adapted from Alcoholics Anonymous and other substance abuse organizations; this group is only for teens and those who love them.

http://www.teensurfer.com/drugalc.htm The straight facts about what each drug does, doesn't do, and the danger involved

http://www.TLCGirls.org Temporary treatment and live-in center for adolescent girls *http://www.wildernessaltschool.com* A 60 day in-patient wilderness treatment center for males ages 14-24.

*911 Emergency number for ambulance, police and all other crisis.

Alcohol Abuse and Crisis Intervention (talks about all drugs) 800 234 0246 Focuses on how to get help and health care

Alcoholics Anonymous Inter-Group 212 647-1680 Support groups for recovering alcoholics; look in your local phone book under AA for the number nearest to you; names are never asked and like their name says all information remains nameless.

*American Council for Drug Education 800 Drughelp, 800 488 Drug, 800 Cocaine, 800 9-Heroin, 800 Relapse, 888 marijuana; help available not only for those who live with an addict but for the addicts themselves

American Council on Alcoholism 800 527-5344 helpline

*Association of American Indian Physicians 405 946 7072

The Caron Foundation 215 678-2332 A nonprofit addiction and chemically dependency treatment center providing services for adults and adolescents

*Child Abuse Hotline—800 422-4453 Child help

*Children of Alcoholics Foundation 800 359-COAF Immediate crisis help information

*Families Anonymous 800 736-9805 10AM to 4PM Monday through Friday Western time. Excellent support group for families struggling with substance abuse issues; all ages are welcomed at their meetings

*Gam-Anon International Services 718 352-1671 Tuesday 9AM to 4:30 PM and Thursdays 9AM to 5 PM Eastern time; Will help families who live with gamblers find a self-help group near them or help you start one.

Gamblers Anonymous International Service Office 213 386-8789 Has a list of organizations near you;

*Hazelden Foundation 800 257-7810 or 800 257-7800 A non-profit organization dedicated to helping people recover from alcoholism and drug addiction; it also offers programs for families who live with an active substance abuser or with a recovered addict

*Indian Health Service (NCADD) 301 443-4297 or 505 837 4121

Lowe Family Foundation 203 362-4883 For families coping with alcoholism

Marijuana Anonymous 800 766 6779 Look also in your local phone book for a number in your area; support group to help each other recover from marijuana addiction.

*Nar Anon Family Groups 310 547-5800 Look also in your local phone book for a number in your area; support groups for family and friends of drug abusers.

Narcotics Anonymous 818 773-9999 Look also in your local phone book for a number in your area; support groups for recovering drug abusers and those who want to abstain from drugs

*National Al-Anon and Alateen 800 356-9996, 800 344-2666 Look in your phone book for local Al-Anon and Alateen groups; known for helping families who live with alcoholics regain their lives;

*National Association for Children of Alcoholics (and drug abusers) 888-554-COAS

*National Association of Native American Children of Alcoholics 206 467-7686

*National Boys Town Line (also for girls) 800 448-3000 A telephone counselor is available day or night

*National Clearinghouse for Alcohol and Drug Information 800 729-6686 press #2 to talk to an advisor about help in your area

National Intervention Network 800 654 HOPE provides information on family intervention

National Peer Helpers Association 913 362 0794 Resources you need to develop and nurture successful peer programs

*National Youth Crisis hotline 800 448-4663 Telephone counselors will listen to you and help you

*NCADD (National Council On Alcoholism and Drug Dependence, Inc.) 800 NCA-CALL Answers all kinds of questions about alcoholism, other drug dependencies and where the substance abusers and those living with them can seek help

Partners 312 988-51 45 A relationship education course offered in schools nationwide or write for a brochure to American Bar Association/ Family Law Section, 750 North Lake Shore Drive, Chicago, Illinois 60611

*Rain (national network for rape, abuse, incest victims) 800 656
4673 Counselors answer the phone

The Bureau For At-Risk Youth 1 800 99-YOUTH User-friendly
videos, programs, publications about addiction and living with
addiction

*Youth Suicide And Runaway 800 999-9999 An excellent 24-hour
hotline available seven days a week

Epilogue

REMEMBER THAT YOU are not alone.
Remember that there is a lot you can do with your life.
Remember that you do not have to be a prisoner of your circumstances.

Your aim in part should be to establish for yourself a healthy lifestyle. Be realistic in your expectations of your family and plan time with people whose healthy lifestyles you enjoy. Find ways to relieve your stress by sports, working out, talking to friends, and joining groups. I know that I mentioned groups and groups, counseling and counseling, over and over again in this book. Sometimes one needs help. Did you ever hear of someone setting his or her broken leg? No. You go for help. Our spirits, our emotions are just as tender as a broken leg. Maybe more so. Truly these groups are your lifeline to a good and a worthwhile life.

Edith Lynn Hornik-Beer